VEGETARIAN
ENTERTAINING

cooking is one of those lovely things.

VEGETARIAN ENTERTAINING

MATTHEW DRENNAN
AND ANNIE NICHOLS

Select
Editions

This edition published in 1998 by
Select Editions
Vancouver, Canada
Ph: 1 (604) 415-2444

ISBN 1-896639-30-5

© Anness Publishing Limited 1997

Produced by Anness Publishing Limited
Hermes House, 88-89 Blackfriars Road
London SE1 8HA

Publisher: Joanna Lorenz
Senior Cookery Editor: Linda Fraser
In-house Editor: Margaret Malone
Designer: Brian Weldon
Photographers: Karl Adamson, Edward Allwright, James Duncan
and Amanda Heywood
Recipes: Matthew Drennan and Annie Nichols
Additional Recipes: Shirley Gill, Carole Handslip and Steven Wheeler
Stylists: Madeleine Brehaut and Hilary Guy

Previously published as individual titles in the *Step-by-Step* series.

Printed in Hong Kong / China

1 3 5 7 9 10 8 6 4 2

CONTENTS

INTRODUCTION

Today, vegetarian food is a familiar part of everyday cuisine. The notion that vegetarian dishes are uninspiring, heavy and dull has long been dispelled. For many of us, vegetarian food is the perfect solution when quick, light, mid-week standbys are needed. *Vegetarian Entertaining,* however, provides the home cook with a host of delectable ideas for entertaining, with recipes suitable for every occasion from informal relaxed meals through to more sumptuous events.

With the growth of vegetarianism we have discovered the joy of cooking with foods such as grains, beans and vegetables, and *Vegetarian Entertaining* demonstrates how easy it can be to produce a complete vegetarian lunch or dinner menu that looks good, tastes delicious and is also simple and easy to prepare. All the recipes combine freshly prepared produce with staples from the pantry or freezer and utilize the proliferation of new and exotic herbs and spices now readily available, making it possible to create exciting and imaginative dishes with ease.

The secret of success when entertaining is to make sure you have all the ingredients and necessary equipment before you begin. Advice on stocking the pantry and what constitutes a survival kitchen is given on the next few pages. Decide on your menu as early as possible, and work out what preparations can be done beforehand. The menu planner section provides some useful suggestions for combining appropriate appetizers, main courses, salads and desserts. Master the 'all hands on deck' method, using the time while one item is cooking to prepare the next, and you may be surprised to discover just how easy it can be to cook a number of dishes and still enjoy the occasion.

So, whether you are entertaining with family and friends or planning a more formal meal, this book shows you how to plan and cook a complete vegetarian menu that is both delicious and easy to prepare – leaving you with more time to spend with your guests. Fully illustrated with step-by-step instructions, *Vegetarian Entertaining* ensures that you will never be short of a perfect and tempting dish for every special occasion.

The Pantry

Your pantry should be the backbone of your kitchen. Stock it sensibly, and you'll always have the means to make a tasty, satisfying meal. Begin with the basics and expand as you experiment, buying small quantities whenever possible and keeping an eye on "sell by" dates.

OILS, SAUCES AND CANNED GOODS

Chili oil
Use this fiery oil sparingly to liven up vegetable stir-fries and similar dishes.

Olive oil
If you must have only one oil, a good olive oil will suit most purposes (except deep-frying). Extra virgin olive oil is more expensive and best kept for salads.

Peanut oil
This bland-tasting oil will not mask delicate flavors. It is good for deep-frying. Use vegetable or sunflower oil instead, if you prefer.

Sesame oil
Favored in oriental cooking for its flavor, this rich oil can be used on its own or combined with vegetable oil.

Ghee
This is pure clarified butter used in Indian cooking. Make your own or substitute vegetable, corn or nut oil.

Black bean sauce
A thick aromatic sauce made from beans, used for marinades and stir-fries.

Passata/Strained tomatoes
This is a thick sauce made from strained tomatoes, used mainly in Italian cooking.

Soy sauce
A thin, salty, black liquid made from fermented soy beans. Add a splash at the end of cooking and offer extra at the table.

Sun-dried tomatoes
These deliciously sweet tomatoes, baked in the sun and dried, are sold in bags or in jars, steeped in olive oil.

Tahini
Made from ground sesame seeds, this paste is used in Middle Eastern cookery.

Tomato paste
This is a concentrated tomato sauce which is sold in cans, jars or tubes. A version made from sun-dried tomatoes is also now available.

Canned beans, lentils, peas
Chick-peas, cannellini beans, green lentils, haricot beans and red kidney beans survive the canning process well. Wash in cold running water, and drain well before use.

Canned vegetables
Although fresh vegetables are best for most cooking, some canned products are very useful. Artichoke hearts have a mild sweet flavor and are great for adding to stir-fries, salads or risottos. Pimientos are whole red bell peppers in jars, seeded and peeled. Use them for stews and soups, but stick to fresh bell peppers for anything else as they lack the firmness of bite that is needed for dishes such as stir-fries. Canned tomatoes are an essential ingredient to have in the pantry. There is now a very wide range available, whole or chopped, plain or with herbs, spices or other flavorings. Additional useful items to include are corn kernels, or ratatouille (found in specialty stores in jars, or at deli counters).

chick-peas

tahini

tomato paste

maple syrup

red wine

chili sauce

chopped
tomatoes

chili
oil

herb vinegar

black olive
paste

pimientos

corn

white wine
vinegar

ratatouille

kidney beans

lentils

chilies in oil

tabini

plum tomatoes

soy sauce

black bean
sauce

olive
oil

mustard

honey

strained
tomatoes

peanut
oil

red wine
vinegar

balsamic
vinegar

ghee

salad dressing

black olives

Dry Goods

Assuming your pantry already includes flours, sugars and dried fruits, the following items are invaluable for speedy cooking. The list of spices relates specifically to the recipes in this book.

Bulgur
This whole wheat grain is steam-dried and cracked before sale, so only needs a brief soaking before use. Keep it cool and dry in the pantry and it will last for a few months.

Nuts
Buy nuts in small quantities and store in a dry place. Almonds, cashews, peanuts, pecans, pine nuts and walnuts all feature prominently in this book.

Pasta
While fresh pasta is generally preferred, both for flavor and for speed of cooking, the dried product is a very valuable pantry ingredient. Spaghetti, noodles (Italian and oriental) and shapes are all useful.

Rice
If you stock only one type of rice, make it basmati, which has a superior flavor and fragrance. A mixture of basmati and wild rice (not a true rice, but the seeds of an aquatic grass) works well.

SPICES

Caraway seeds
Small greenish-brown seeds with a nutty texture and a flavor reminiscent of anise or fennel.

Chinese five-spice powder
Made from a mixture of anise pepper, cassia, fennel seed, star anise and cloves, this spice has an enticing anise (licorice) flavor.

Garam masala
This is an aromatic mixture of different spices used widely in Indian dishes. It is usually added at the end of cooking.

Ground cardamom
Fragrant, with a spicy undertone, cardamom is used in sweet and savory dishes.

Ground coriander
With a warm savory aroma, this spice imparts a mildly hot yet sweetish flavor.

Ground cinnamon
A sweet, fragrant spice ground from the dried rolled inner bark of a tropical tree.

Ground cumin
Sweet and pungent, with a unique and distinctive taste.

Ground turmeric
With a somewhat musty flavor and aroma, this spice adds a deep yellow color to food. It is sometimes used in place of saffron to add color, although it does not have the same flavor.

Saffron
This is the most expensive spice in the world. It has a pungent scent with a slightly bittersweet taste. The threads are crushed and steeped in a little liquid before use.

rice

ground turmeric

ground cumin

caraway seed

egg noodles

nuts

penne

bulgur

pecan nuts

garam masala

dried chilies

spaghetti

cornstarch

mixed spice

black peppercorns

Chinese five-spice powder

pine nuts

poppy seeds

chili powder

ground coriander

sea salt

thyme

cumin seed

sugar

long grain rice

granulated sugar

garlic

Fresh Fruit and Vegetables

Thanks to the amazing range of fresh produce now available, the vegetarian repertoire has expanded enormously. Filled with complex carbohydrates, protein, vitamins and minerals, fresh fruit and vegetables are essential to a healthy vegetarian diet.

Alfalfa sprouts
These crisp, sprouting seeds with a delicious nutty flavor are highly nutritious and rich in protein, fiber, vitamins and minerals.

Baby corn
These young corn are most delicious when lightly cooked, so are especially suitable for stir-fries.

Broad beans
The plump inner bean is delicious when lightly steamed, and makes a good accompaniment to richly flavored foods.

Celeriac
This underrated vegetable has a delicious, sweet, celery-like flavor.

Chilies
There are hundreds of varieties of these hot relatives of the capsicum family. They should be treated with caution. When preparing chillies take special care to avoid rubbing your eyes or face as their juices can irritate the skin.

Fennel
A crisp, delicious, sweet aniseed-flavored vegetable, which can be eaten raw, finely sliced, or cooked. Add a little to vegetable stock for an unusual extra flavoring.

Limes
Fresh and sharp with an intense sour flavor.

Okra
Okra lends a creamy, silky consistency to vegetable dishes.

Patty pan squash
These lovely, scallop-edged baby squash have a similar flavor to zucchini.

Peas
Sweet, tender peas, popped fresh from the pod are unbeatable. Make the most of them when in season.

Pumpkins
There are many different varieties of these members of the gourd family. A thick tough skin belies the fragrant, pale or bright orange flesh within.

Red onions
Mild and sweeter than most onions, their purple flesh makes a pretty addition to any vegetable dish.

Sweet potatoes
The skin of these tubers can be pinkish or brown and the flesh varies from creamy white to yellow or pale orange. Despite its name, this vegetable is not related to the everyday potato. The sweet potato usually has an elongated shape, although some round varieties are available.

Tomatoes
Recent demand for full-flavored tomatoes means that many varieties now abound, from the sweet little cherry tomatoes, to the plump Italian plum and the large beefsteak tomatoes.

Turnips
Sweet, nutty-flavored turnips range from the walnut-sized baby roots (that are often sold still attached to their green tops) to large mature turnips.

fennel

okra

turnips

pumpkin

celeriac

tomatoes

chillies

broad beans

plum tomatoes

cherry tomatoes

sweet potatoes

peas

alfalfa sprouts

red onions

patty pan squash

limes

baby sweetcorn

Pasta, Beans and Grains

Pasta, beans and grains all belong to the important complex carbohydrate group. Most are low in fat and contain plenty of vitamins, minerals and dietary fibre.

Adzuki beans
A small, reddish brown, shiny bean with a unique strong nutty, sweet flavor.

Arborio rice
One of the best and most commonly available rices to use for risotto.

Basmati rice and brown basmati rice
Harvested from the foothills of the Himalayas with a very distinctive, fragrant aroma.

Black-eyed beans
Sometimes referred to as black-eyed peas, these small beans with a black spot have a savory flavor and succulent texture.

Bulgur wheat
A whole wheat grain that is steamed-dried and cracked so it only needs brief soaking before use.

Campanelle
A pretty frilled, twisted pasta tube.

Cannellini beans
These look like small white kidney beans and belong to the same family. They have a soft texture when cooked.

Capellini
Known as angel-hair pasta, this is a very fine variety.

Chick-peas
These pale golden-brown, hard peas look rather like small dry hazelnuts. They have a rich nutty flavor.

Couscous
Made from coarse semolina, this lovely soft grain is now produced to need only a brief moistening before use.

Egg noodles
The most common of all oriental noodles, they take only minutes to cook.

Flageolet beans
Pale green, long and slim, these are navy beans removed from the pod while young. They have a tender texture when cooked.

Green lentils
This superior lentil is prized for its flavor and texture.

Long-grain rice and brown long-grain rice
Long, translucent grains are valued for their nutty flavor.

Navy or white beans
These oval cream beans are commonly seen as canned baked beans.

Oatmeal
Sliced whole oat grain which is graded from pinhead (the coarsest) to medium and fine (medium is shown here). A good source of calcium, potassium and iron.

Pasta bows
The Italian name for this is *farfalle* or 'butterfly', because of its shape.

Penne
Short, tubular pasta shapes, also known as quills.

Polenta
Fine yellow cornmeal, used to make a soft porridge.

Soup pasta
This tiny pasta comes in many different shapes.

Spaghetti
The most popular pasta, it has long, thin strands.

Tagliatelle
Flat, long ribbon noodles. The green version is flavored with spinach.

Wild rice
Not a true rice but the seed of an aquatic grass. The brown, long grains open when cooked.

spaghetti

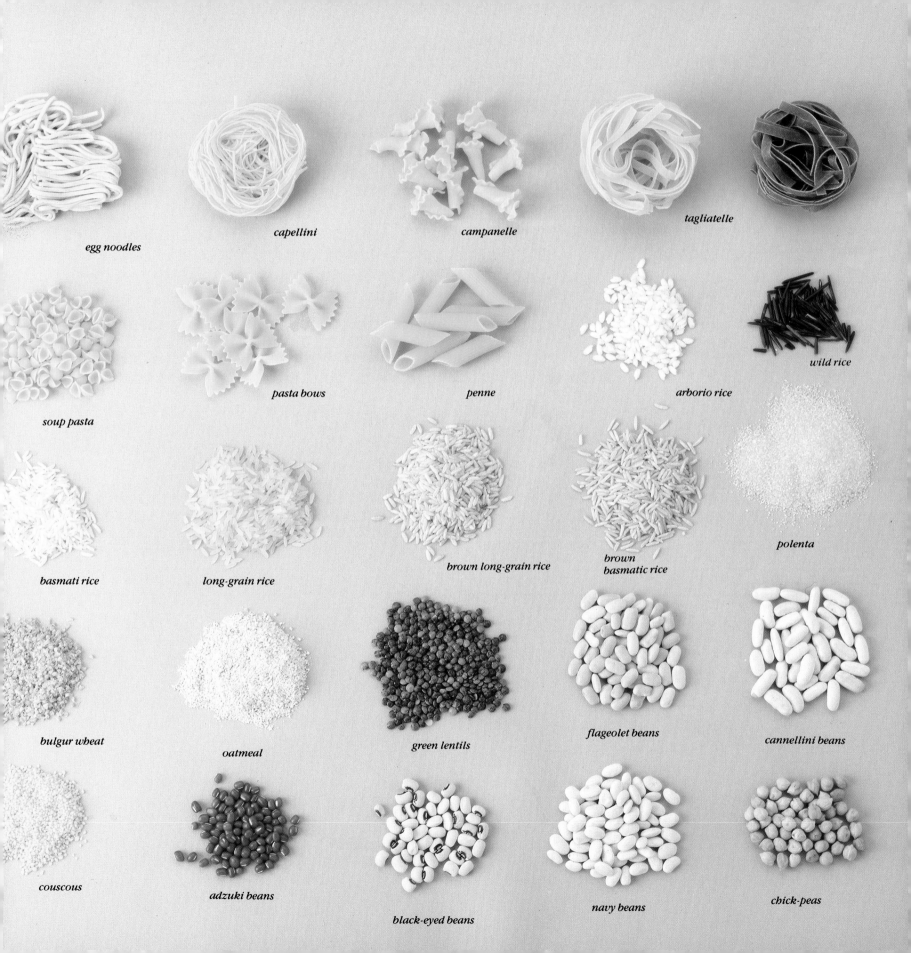

egg noodles

capellini

campanelle

tagliatelle

soup pasta

pasta bows

penne

arborio rice

wild rice

basmati rice

long-grain rice

brown long-grain rice

brown
basmatic rice

polenta

bulgur wheat

oatmeal

green lentils

flageolet beans

cannellini beans

couscous

adzuki beans

black-eyed beans

navy beans

chick-peas

The Vegetarian Kitchen Cupboard

Although not strictly essential, the ingredients listed here will greatly enhance any vegetarian dish, and are convenient to have on hand when preparing food at the last minute.

Balsamic vinegar
A deliciously smooth, rich, sweet-and-sour flavored vinegar made in Modena in northern Italy.

Hazelnut oil
A richly flavored nutty oil. Just a few drops will lift the flavor of a plain salad.

Olive oil
This is high in mono-unsaturated fats and vitamin A. It ranges from the refined pale yellow variety to the rich herbaceous extra-virgin.

Raspberry vinegar
A sweet, light vinegar with the slight tang of raspberries.

Sesame oil
This delicious, rich oil is often used in oriental cuisine as a flavoring rather than as a cooking oil.

Sunflower oil
A mild polyunsaturated oil that is useful for all types of cooking.

Sun-dried tomatoes
A preserved tomato which can be bought either in bags or steeped in olive oil in jars.

Tahini
A paste made from ground sesame seeds, it is widely used in Middle Eastern cooking.

Walnut oil
High in polyunsaturates, this is a delicious nutty oil.

Cheeses and Tofu

Improvements in handling and distribution mean that we are now able to buy a huge range of local and imported cheeses in excellent condition. Tofu, available in various forms, is another valuable source of protein.

Blue cheese
Where a recipe fails to specify a particular blue cheese, use Roquefort if a strong flavor is required and Danish for a milder result.

Camembert
This cheese is made from cow's milk. It has a mild, creamy taste with a slight acidic edge that gets milder with age.

Feta
This soft Greek cheese is rindless, white in color and has a crumbly texture. It is slightly sour, piquant and quite salty to the taste.

Goat cheese
Fresh goat cheese is soft and creamy. As it ages, the cheese becomes harder and the flavor intensifies.

Mozzarella
A unique Italian cheese made from cow's milk, mozzarella has a mild, creamy taste and an unusual spongy texture.

Parmesan
A hard cheese from Italy with a wonderful, distinctive flavor. It is usually grated or shaved wafer-thin. Buy it fresh as the pre-grated cheese sold commercially often lacks the true flavor.

Stilton
An English semi-hard cheese with blue veins, Stilton has a soft, moist texture and a strong flavor.

Tofu
This is an unfermented bean curd made from soy beans. It absorbs flavors readily and is frequently marinated before use. Various forms are available, from soft silken tofu to a firm type which can be cubed and sautéed.

goat cheese

feta

dolcelatte

Stilton

mozzarella

Camembert

Parmesan

Spices and Seasonings

Spices and seasonings are indispensable for enhancing the flavors of foods that might otherwise be bland and lacking in substance.

Allspice
This is available both whole and ground and imparts a flavoring that is like a mixture of nutmeg, cinnamon, cloves and pepper.

Caraway
A pungent and aromatic spice that is widely used in German and Austrian cooking.

Cayenne
Ground from small red chillies, it is extremely spicy, and should be used sparingly.

Cinnamon
Cinnamon is a sweet and fragrant spice ground from the dried, rolled inner bark of a tropical tree that is native to Sri Lanka.

Cloves
A strongly aromatic spice with a slightly bitter taste.

Coriander
A sweet, warm aromatic spice that is used extensively in Indian and South-east Asian cooking.

Cumin
A uniquely flavored spice with a sweetly pungent and very distinctive taste.

Fennel seeds
These seeds have a strong, sweet anise-liquorice flavor.

Ginger
The fresh root has a clean refreshing flavor. Ginger is also available dried and ground.

Green cardamom
The pods should be broken open and the small black seeds ground to fully appreciate the mellow fragrant, slightly spicy aroma.

Juniper berries
These pine-scented, bitter-sweet berries provide the main flavoring of gin.

Lemon grass
A strong clean, refreshing citrus flavoring that is widely used in Thai and Vietnamese cooking.

Nutmeg
A very aromatic spice with a warm, sweet, nutty flavor.

Paprika
The flavor can range from sweet and lightly piquant, to pungent and fiery.

Saffron
This is the most expensive spice in the world, but you need only a tiny amount to flavor and color any dish.

Star anise
A sweet, pungent liquorice-flavored spice that is important in Chinese cooking.

Turmeric
Mainly used for its bright yellow coloring, it has a slightly musty taste and aroma.

Yellow mustard seeds
Less pungent than brown or black mustard seeds, they have a sweet, mild piquancy.

fennel seeds

star anise

cayenne

ginger

green cardamom

ground cloves

cloves

ground nutmeg

nutmeg

ground coriander

coriander seeds

ground cumin

cumin seeds

allspice berries

ground allspice

ground turmeric

ground cinnamon

ground ginger

caraway seeds

juniper berries

yellow mustard seeds

cinnamon sticks

saffron

lemon grass

paprika

Nuts

Nuts provide a healthy source of energy, and are rich in fiber, protein, vitamins B and E and several minerals. However, they are high in fats (though mostly mono- and polyunsaturated) so are usually also high in calories.

pecans

Almonds
There are two types, sweet and bitter, the bitter type being poisonous when eaten raw. This delicious nut enriches many dishes and is especially high in protein.

Brazil nuts
As the name would suggest, these nuts originate from the Brazilian Amazon. The high oil content means that these nuts quickly turn rancid.

Chestnuts
Not to be confused with the horse-chestnut, these softer textured nuts are low in fat and high in carbohydrates. They can be bought fresh, canned (whole or puréed), vacuum-packed and dried.

Hazelnuts
These wonderfully aromatic sweet nuts add flavor to both sweet and savory dishes. Roasting adds more flavor.

Peanuts
Not strictly a true nut, these most popular of nuts have a distinctive flavor and are rich in protein.

Pecans
A native of the USA, these are sweet and richly flavored nuts similar to walnuts.

Pine nuts
These soft, creamy colored nuts are found at the base of a species of pine cone. They have a delicate flavor.

Pistachios
These are richly flavored with a bright green coloring.

Walnuts
The most versatile of all nuts, walnuts impart a rich full flavor.

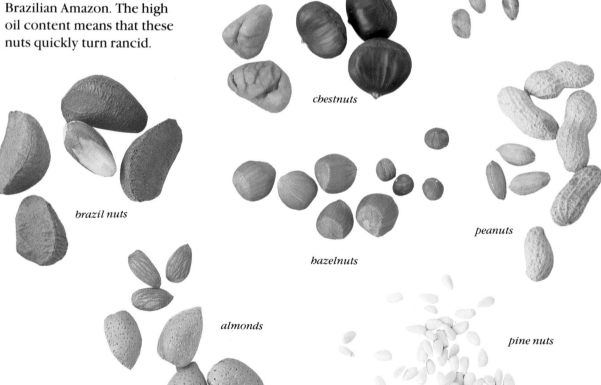

brazil nuts

chestnuts

pistachios

almonds

hazelnuts

peanuts

pine nuts

walnuts

Flours

Flour can be ground from grains, cereals, seeds, nuts and even roots and tubers.

Buckwheat flour
A non-wheat flour, ground from the seed of a plant that is related to rhubarb. It has a strong nutty flavor and is rich in vitamins A and B, calcium and carbohydrate.

White flour
This contains 75 per cent or less of the wheat grain so is not as nutritious as wholewheat flour.

Wholewheat flour
Ground from the entire whole grain it is rich in protein, vitamins and fibre, so is highly nutritious.

Seeds

Seeds provide a rich source of protein, fiber, vitamins, minerals and starch.

Poppy seeds
These mild, sweet seeds come from the opium poppy, but are free from narcotic properties.

Pumpkin seeds
From the vegetable of the same name, these flat green seeds have a light, distinctive flavor and are rich in zinc, protein and iron.

Sesame seeds
These tiny, light brown or creamy colored seeds have a mild, sweet nutty flavor and are rich in protein and calcium.

Sunflower seeds
These seeds have a distinctive flavor and they are rich in protein, fiber, iron and calcium.

white flour

buckwheat flour

sunflower seeds

wholewheat flour

pumpkin seeds

poppy seeds

sesame seeds

Equipment

Stocking up on every item in your local cookware store will not make you a better cook, but some basic items are definitely worth investing in.

A few good saucepans in various sizes and with tight-fitting lids are a must. Heavy-bottomed and nonstick pans are best. A large nonstick frying pan is invaluable for the quick cook. The food cooks faster when spread over a wider surface area. For the same reason, a good wok is essential. I suggest using a large saucepan or frying pan when the recipe calls for occasional stirring, and a wok for continuous movement, such as stir-frying.

Good-quality knives can halve your preparation time, but more importantly, a really sharp knife is safer than a blunt one. You can do yourself a lot of damage if your hand slips when you are pressing down hard with a blunt knife. For basic, day-to-day use, choose a good chopping knife, a small vegetable knife and a long, serrated bread knife. If possible, store knives safely in well-secured, slotted racks. Drawer storage is not good for knives as the blades can easily become damaged when they are knocked around. If you do have to keep knives in a drawer, make sure they are stored with their handles toward the front for safe lifting and keep the blades protected in some way. Good, sharp knives are essential and indispensable pieces of kitchen equipment, so it is worth taking care of them.

A few of the recipes in this book call for the use of a food processor or blender, which does save time and effort but is not strictly necessary. Some essential pieces of kitchen equipment which almost seem too obvious to mention, include chopping boards, a colander, a strainer, a grater, a whisk and some means of extracting citrus juice, be this a squeezer or a juicer.

For the cook who likes to cook speedily and efficiently, where you store your equipment is an important factor to consider. I use my stove as the pivot around which most of the action takes place. Pots, pans, whisks, spoons and strainers hang conveniently overhead within easy reach, a chopping board is on an adjacent work surface, and ceramic pots hold a variety of wooden spoons, spatulas, ladles, scissors, peelers and other kitchen utensils, again all within easy reach.

wooden spatula

ladle

scissors

knives and peelers

vegetable knife

bread knife

whisks

slotted spoon

grater

serving spoon

colander

chopping board

wok

saucepans

frying pan

TECHNIQUES

Once mastered, the techniques described here will help you to prepare vegetables speedily and with less waste, to produce better results with ease.

Peeling and Seeding Tomatoes

A simple and efficient way of preparing tomatoes.

1 Use a sharp knife to cut a small cross on the bottom of the tomato.

2 Turn the tomato over and cut out the core.

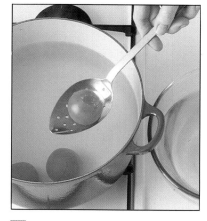

3 Immerse the tomato in boiling water for 10–15 seconds, then transfer to a bowl of cold water using a slotted spoon.

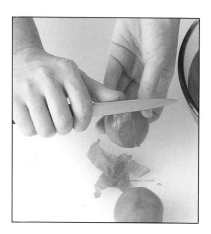

4 Lift out the tomato and peel (the skin should be easy to remove).

5 Cut the tomato in half crosswise and squeeze out the seeds.

6 Use a large knife to cut the peeled tomato into strips, then chop across the strips to make dice.

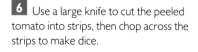

Chopping Onions

Uniform-sized dice make cooking easy. This method can't be beaten.

1 Peel the onion. Cut it in half with a large knife and set it cut-side down on a board. Make lengthwise vertical cuts along the onion, cutting almost but not quite through to the root.

2 Make 2 horizontal cuts from the stalk and towards the root, but not through it.

3 Cut the onion crosswise to form small, even dice.

Slicing Onions

Use thin slices for sautéeing or to flavor oils for stir-frying, or use sweet onion slices in salads.

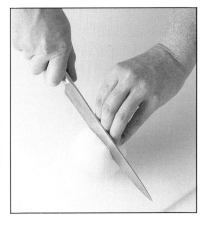

1 Peel the onion. Cut it in half with a large knife and set it cut-side down on a chopping board.

2 Cut out a triangular piece of the core from each half.

3 Cut across each half in vertical slices.

Shredding Cabbage

This method is useful for coleslaws, pickled cabbage or any cooked dish.

1 Use a large knife to cut the cabbage into quarters.

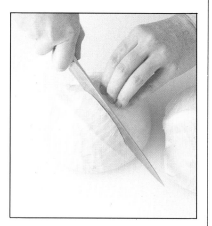

2 Cut out the core from each quarter.

3 Slice across each quarter to form fine, even shreds.

Cutting Carrot Julienne

Thin julienne strips of any vegetable make decorative accompaniments, or can be used in stir-fries.

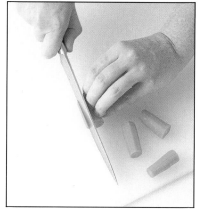

1 Peel the carrot and use a large knife to cut it into 2 in lengths. Cut a thin sliver from one side of each piece so that it sits flat on the board.

2 Cut into thin lengthwise slices.

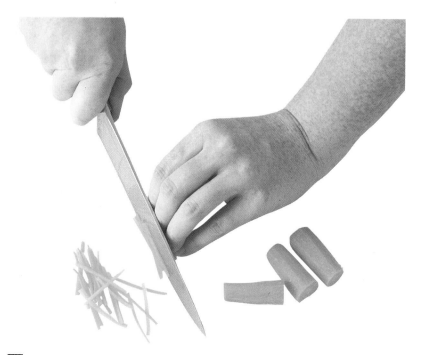

3 Stack the slices and cut through them to make fine strips.

Chopping Fresh Ginger

Fresh ginger imparts a clean, refreshing taste. Follow the instructions to chop finely.

1 Break off small knobs of ginger from the main root and peel.

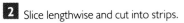

2 Slice lengthwise and cut into strips.

3 Cut across the strips to form small, even dice.

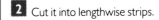

Chopping Chilies

Fresh chilies must be handled with care. Always work in a well-ventilated area and keep away from your eyes.

1 Cut the chili in half lengthwise and remove the core and seeds.

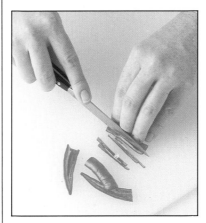

2 Cut it into lengthwise strips.

3 Cut across the strips to form small, even dice.

Make a Meal of it

The recipes in this book have been specially chosen as they can be served alone with a simple side order of pasta, rice or potatoes, or they can easily be combined together to form delicious menus, perfect for entertaining. The ease and speed of preparation that is common to them all, makes these dishes the perfect choice for entertaining, as they provide the cook with more time to enjoy the company instead of being confined to the kitchen. On the following pages you can choose to combine favorite main course dishes of your choice with the simple-to-make appetizers and desserts featured, or select from the complete menus provided featuring appropriate dishes for every stage of the meal.

APPETIZERS

Lightly poached asparagus with sour cream and lemon.

Warm focaccia bread accompanied by olive oil, Kosher salt and black olives.

Broiled cherry tomatoes served with salad and basil leaves, drizzled with a little dressing.

Crudités of celery, carrot, baby corn and snow peas served with mayonnaise with a little pesto stirred through.

Thin slices of French bread, topped with tapenade (black olive paste) and mozzarella, then broiled and served hot.

Pre-made hummus and tzatziki served as dips with strips of warm pita bread and black olives.

Chopped fresh tomatoes and onion flavored with chopped fresh cilantro, and served with poppadums.

DESSERTS

Slices of sticky ginger cake warmed through in the microwave and served with a little maple syrup and cream.

Fresh summer berries, sprinkled with Kirsch and vanilla sugar, served with sour cream or plain yogurt.

Sweetened, whipped cream flavored with passionfruit and served on banana slices. Add amaretti biscuits for contrast.

A slice of Swiss roll topped with a scoop of ice cream, covered in stiff meringue and broiled until golden.

Banana slices and orange segments topped with a little apricot jam, wrapped in foil and baked in a hot oven for 10 minutes. Serve with cream.

Fresh blackberries crushed lightly with a fork and gently folded into softly whipped cream. Add a drizzle of Cassis (optional) and sugar to taste.

Brandy-snap baskets filled with raspberries and peach slices, topped with a swirl of cream and a sprig of mint.

Ripe plums, halved, sprinkled with brandy and filled with mascarpone cheese. The plums are topped with chopped nuts and brown sugar, then broiled until the sugar has melted.

Menus for Entertaining

When you have guests to feed, clever combining of well-chosen dishes can quickly result in an impressive menu in next to no time. The menu suggestions below feature main course vegetarian meals, quick and easy appetizers, salads and desserts, specially chosen for their ease of preparation and tastiness.

Menu 1

Warm focaccia bread with Kosher salt and olives

Asparagus Rolls with Herb Butter Sauce

Lentil Stir-fry served with a green salad

Summer berries with Kirsch and vanilla sugar

Menu 2

Broiled cherry tomato and basil salad

Mushrooms with Leeks and Stilton

Potato, Broccoli and Red Bell Pepper Stir-fry

Baked banana and orange segments

Menu 3

Poached asparagus with crème fraîche and lemon

Crusty Rolls with Zucchini and Saffron

Red Fried Rice

Warm ginger cake with maple syrup

Menu 4

French bread slices with tapenade and mozzarella

Lemon and Parmesan Cappellini with Herb Bread

Fresh Spinach and Avocado Salad

Banana and amaretti with passionfruit cream

Menu 5

Fresh tomato and cilantro with poppadoms

Bengali-style Vegetables

Cumin-spiced Large Zucchini and Spinach

Spiced potato and cauliflower
Fresh fruit

Menu 6

Crudités with mayonnaise dip

Potato, Spinach and Pine Nut Gratin

Vegetable Kebabs with Mustard and Honey

Broiled mascarpone plums

Melon and Basil Soup

A deliciously refreshing, chilled fruit soup, just right for a hot summer's day.

Serves 4–6

INGREDIENTS
2 canteloupe or honeydew melons
⅓ cup superfine sugar
¾ cup water
finely grated zest and juice of 1 lime
3 tbsp shredded fresh basil
fresh basil leaves, to garnish

basil

sugar

lime

melon

1 Cut the melons in half across the middle. Scrape out the seeds and discard. Using a melon baller, scoop out 20–24 balls and set aside for the garnish. Scoop out the remaining flesh and place in a blender or food processor.

2 Place the sugar, water and lime zest in a small pan over a low heat. Stir until dissolved, bring to the boil and simmer for 2–3 minutes. Remove from the heat and leave to cool slightly. Pour half the mixture into the blender or food processor with the melon flesh. Blend until smooth, adding the remaining syrup and lime juice to taste.

3 Pour the mixture into a bowl, stir in the basil and chill. Serve garnished with basil leaves and melon balls.

COOK'S TIP
Add the syrup in two stages, as the amount of sugar needed will depend on the sweetness of the melon.

Leek, Parsnip and Ginger Soup

A flavorful winter warmer, with the added spiciness of fresh ginger.

Serves 4–6

INGREDIENTS
2 tbsp olive oil
8 oz leeks, sliced
2 tbsp finely chopped fresh ginger root
1 ½ lb parsnips, roughly chopped
1 ¼ cups dry white wine, such as Sauvignon blanc
5 cups vegetable stock or water
salt and freshly ground black pepper
low-fat ricotta cheese, to garnish
paprika, to garnish

ginger

parsnip

vegetable stock

leeks

1 Heat the oil in a large pan and add the leeks and ginger. Cook gently for 2–3 minutes, until the leeks start to soften.

2 Add the parsnips and cook for a further 7–8 minutes.

3 Pour in the wine and stock or water and bring to the boil. Reduce the heat and simmer for 20–30 minutes or until the parsnips are tender.

4 Purée in a blender until smooth. Season to taste. Reheat and garnish with a swirl of ricotta cheese and a light dusting of paprika.

Chilled Fresh Tomato Soup

This effortless uncooked soup can be made in minutes.

Serves 4–6

INGREDIENTS

3–3½ lb ripe tomatoes, peeled and
   roughly chopped
4 garlic cloves, crushed
2 tbsp extra-virgin olive oil (optional)
2 tbsp balsamic vinegar
freshly ground black pepper
4 slices wholewheat bread
low-fat ricotta cheese, to garnish

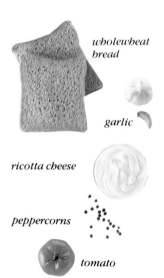

*wholewheat
bread*

garlic

ricotta cheese

peppercorns

tomato

COOK'S TIP

For the best flavor, it is important to
use only fully ripened, succulent
tomatoes in this soup.

1 Place the tomatoes in a blender with
the garlic and olive oil if using. Blend until
smooth.

2 Pass the mixture through a sieve to
remove the seeds. Stir in the balsamic
vinegar and season to taste with pepper.
Leave in the fridge to chill.

3 Toast the bread lightly on both sides.
While still hot, cut off the crusts and slice
in half horizontally. Place the toast on a
board with the uncooked sides facing
down and, using a circular motion, rub to
remove any doughy pieces of bread.

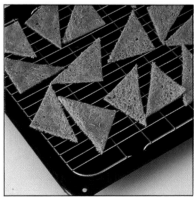

4 Cut each slice into 4 triangles. Place
on a griddle and toast the uncooked sides
until lightly golden. Garnish each bowl of
soup with a spoonful of ricotta cheese and
serve with the melba toast.

Broccoli and Almond Soup

The creaminess of the toasted almonds combines perfectly with the slight bitterness of the taste of broccoli.

Serves 4–6

INGREDIENTS
⅔ cup ground almonds
1½ lb broccoli
3¾ cups fresh vegetable stock or
    water
1¼ cups skim or low-fat milk
salt and freshly ground black pepper

ground almonds

skim milk

1 Preheat the oven to 350°F. Spread the ground almonds evenly on a cookie sheet and toast in the oven for about 10 minutes, or until just golden. Reserve ¼ of the almonds and set aside for the garnish.

broccoli

2 Cut the broccoli into small florets and steam for 6–7 minutes or until tender.

3 Place the remaining toasted almonds, broccoli, stock or water and milk in a blender and blend until smooth. Season to taste.

4 Reheat the soup and serve sprinkled with the reserved toasted almonds.

Red Onion and Beet Soup

This beautiful vivid ruby-red soup will look stunning at any dinner party.

Serves 4–6

INGREDIENTS
1 tbsp olive oil
12 oz red onions, sliced
2 garlic cloves, crushed
10 oz cooked beets, cut into
  thin sticks
5 cups fresh vegetable stock or water
1 cup cooked soup pasta
2 tbsp raspberry vinegar
salt and freshly ground black pepper
low-fat yogurt or ricotta cheese, to
  garnish
snipped chives, to garnish

garlic

red onion

beets

pasta

chives

1 Heat the olive oil and add the onions and garlic.

2 Cook gently for about 20 minutes or until soft and tender.

3 Add the beets, stock or water, cooked pasta shapes and vinegar and heat through. Season to taste.

4 Ladle into bowls. Top each one with a spoonful of yogurt or ricotta cheese and sprinkle with chives.

COOK'S TIP

Try substituting cooked barley for the pasta to give extra nuttiness.

Cauliflower, Flageolet and Fennel Seed Soup

The sweet, anise-liquorice flavor of the fennel seeds gives a delicious edge to this hearty soup.

Serves 4–6

INGREDIENTS
1 tbsp olive oil
1 garlic clove, crushed
1 onion, chopped
2 tsp fennel seeds
1 cauliflower, cut into small florets
2 × 14 oz cans flageolet beans,
    drained and rinsed
5 cups fresh vegetable stock or water
salt and freshly ground black pepper
chopped fresh parsley, to garnish
toasted slices of French bread, to
    serve

flageolet beans

French bread

onion

garlic

cauliflower

fennel seeds

parsley

1 Heat the olive oil. Add the garlic, onion and fennel seeds and cook gently for 5 minutes or until softened.

2 Add the cauliflower, half of the beans and the stock or water.

3 Bring to a boil. Reduce the heat and simmer for 10 minutes or until the cauliflower is tender.

4 Pour the soup into a blender and blend until smooth. Stir in the remaining beans and season to taste. Reheat and pour into bowls. Sprinkle with chopped parsley and serve with toasted slices of French bread.

Cucumber and Alfalfa Tortillas

Wheat tortillas are extremely simple to prepare at home. Served with a crisp, fresh salsa, they make a marvelous light lunch or supper dish.

COOK'S TIP

When peeling the avocado be sure to scrape off the bright green flesh from immediately under the skin as this gives the sauce its vivid green color.

Serves 4

INGREDIENTS
2 cups flour, sifted
pinch of salt
3 tbsp olive oil
½–⅔ cup warm water
lime wedges, to garnish

FOR THE SALSA
1 red onion, finely chopped
1 fresh red chilli, seeded and finely chopped
2 tbsp chopped fresh dill or coriander
½ cucumber, peeled and chopped
6 oz alfalfa sprouts

FOR THE SAUCE
1 large ripe avocado, peeled and pitted
juice of 1 lime
2 tbsp soft goat cheese
pinch of paprika

avocado

goat cheese

red chilli

cucumber

dill   *alfalfa sprouts*

1 Mix all the salsa ingredients together in a bowl and set aside.

2 To make the sauce, place the avocado, lime juice and goat cheese in a food processor or blender and blend until smooth. Place in a bowl and cover with plastic wrap. Dust with paprika just before serving.

3 To make the tortillas, place the flour and salt in a food processor, add the oil and blend. Gradually add the water (the amount will vary depending on the type of flour). Stop adding water when a stiff dough has formed. Turn out onto a floured board and knead until smooth. Cover with a damp cloth.

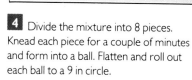

4 Divide the mixture into 8 pieces. Knead each piece for a couple of minutes and form into a ball. Flatten and roll out each ball to a 9 in circle.

5 Heat an ungreased cast-iron pan. Cook 1 tortilla at a time for about 30 seconds on each side. Place the cooked tortillas in a clean dish-towel and repeat until you have 8 tortillas.

6 To serve, spread each tortilla with a spoonful of avocado sauce, top with salsa and roll up. Garnish with lime wedges.

Baked Herb Crêpes

These mouth-watering, light herb crêpes make a striking starter at a dinner party, but are equally splendid served with a crisp salad for lunch.

Serves 4

INGREDIENTS
2 tbsp chopped fresh herbs
  (e.g. parsley, thyme, and chervil)
1 tbsp sunflower oil, plus extra for
  frying
½ cup skim milk
3 eggs
¼ cup flour
pinch of salt
1 tbsp olive oil

FOR THE SAUCE
2 tbsp olive oil
1 small onion, chopped
2 garlic cloves, crushed
1 tbsp grated fresh ginger root
1 × 14 oz can chopped tomatoes

FOR THE FILLING
1 lb fresh spinach
¾ cup ricotta cheese
2 tbsp pine nuts, toasted
5 halves sun-dried tomatoes in olive
  oil, drained and chopped
2 tbsp shredded fresh basil
salt, nutmeg and freshly ground black
  pepper
4 egg whites

onion

parsley

ginger root

chopped tomatoes

spinach

sun-dried tomatoes

garlic

nutmeg

thyme

flour

egg

skim milk

2 Heat a small non-stick crêpe or frying pan and add a very small amount of oil. Pour out any excess oil and pour in a ladleful of the batter. Swirl around to cover the base. Cook for 1–2 minutes, turn over and cook the other side. Repeat with the remaining batter to make 8 crêpes.

3 To make the sauce, heat the oil in a small pan. Add the onion, garlic and ginger and cook gently for 5 minutes until softened. Add the tomatoes and cook for a further 10–15 minutes until the mixture thickens. Purée in a blender, sieve and set aside.

1 To make the crêpes, place the herbs and oil in a blender and blend until smooth, pushing down any whole pieces with a spatula. Add the milk, eggs, flour and salt and process again until smooth and pale green. Leave to rest for 30 minutes.

4 To make the filling, wash the spinach, removing any large stalks, and place in a large pan with only the water that clings to the leaves. Cover and cook, stirring once, until the spinach has just wilted. Remove from the heat and refresh in cold water. Place in a sieve or colander, squeeze out the excess water and chop finely. Mix the spinach with the ricotta, pine nuts, sun-dried tomatoes and basil. Season with salt, nutmeg and freshly ground black pepper.

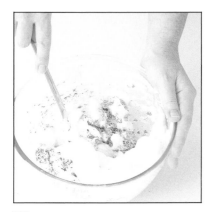

5 Preheat the oven to 375°F. Whisk the 4 egg whites until they form stiff peaks but are not dry. Fold ⅓ into the spinach and ricotta to lighten the mixture, then gently fold in the rest.

6 Taking one crêpe at a time, place on a lightly oiled cookie sheet. Place a large spoonful of filling on each one and fold into quarters. Repeat until all the filling and crêpes are used up. Bake in the oven for 10–15 minutes or until set. Reheat the tomato sauce to serve with the crêpes.

COOK'S TIP
If preferred, use plain sun-dried tomatoes without any oil, and soak them in warm water for 20 minutes before using.

Buckwheat Blinis

These delectable light pancakes originated in Russia. For a special occasion, serve with a small glass of chilled vodka.

Serves 4

INGREDIENTS
1 tsp easy-blend dry yeast
1 cup skim or low-fat milk, warmed
⅓ cup buckwheat flour
⅓ cup flour
2 tsp sugar
pinch of salt
1 egg, separated
oil, for frying

FOR THE AVOCADO CREAM
1 large avocado
⅓ cup low-fat ricotta cheese
juice of 1 lime

FOR THE PICKLED BEETS
8 oz beets
3 tbsp lime juice
snipped chives, to garnish
cracked black peppercorns, to garnish

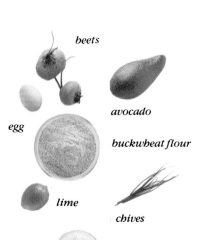

beets
egg
avocado
buckwheat flour
lime
chives
ricotta cheese
skim milk

1 Mix the dry yeast with the milk, then mix with the next 4 ingredients and the egg yolk. Cover with a cloth and leave to prove for about 40 minutes. Whisk the egg white until stiff but not dry and fold into the blini mixture.

2 Heat a little oil in a non-stick pan and add a ladleful of batter to make a 4 in pancake. Cook for 2–3 minutes on each side. Repeat with the remaining batter mixture to make 8 blinis.

3 Cut the avocado in half and remove the pit. Peel and place the flesh in a blender with the ricotta cheese and lime juice. Blend until smooth.

4 Peel the beets and shred finely. Mix with the lime juice. To serve, top each blini with a spoonful of avocado cream. Serve with the pickled beets and garnish with snipped chives and cracked black peppercorns.

Cheese-stuffed Pears

These pears, with their scrumptious creamy topping, make a sublime dish when served with a simple salad.

Serves 4

INGREDIENTS
¼ cup ricotta cheese
¼ cup Saga blue cheese
1 tbsp honey
½ celery stalk, finely sliced
8 green olives, pitted and roughly
  chopped
4 dates, pitted and cut into thin strips
pinch of paprika
4 ripe pears
⅔ cup apple juice

honey

pear

apple juice

dates

Saga blue

celery

olives

COOK'S TIP
Choose ripe pears in season such as Bartlett or Comice.

1 Preheat the oven to 400°F. Place the ricotta in a bowl and crumble in the Saga blue cheese. Add the rest of the ingredients except for the pears and apple juice and mix well.

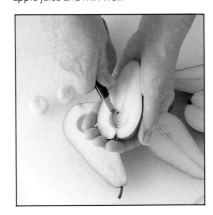

2 Halve the pears lengthwise and use a melon baller to remove the cores. Place in a ovenproof dish and divide the filling equally between them.

3 Pour in the apple juice and cover the dish with foil. Bake for 20 minutes or until the pears are tender.

4 Remove the foil and place the dish under a hot broiler for 3 minutes. Serve immediately.

Soufflé Omelette

This delectable soufflé omelette is light and delicate enough to melt in your mouth.

Serves 1

INGREDIENTS
2 eggs, separated
2 tbsp cold water
1 tbsp chopped fresh coriander
salt and freshly ground black pepper
½ tbsp olive oil
2 tbsp mango chutney
¼ cup Jarlsberg or Swiss cheese, grated

Jarlsberg

mango chutney

eggs

coriander

COOK'S TIP

A light hand is essential to the success of this dish. Do not overmix the egg whites into the yolks or the mixture will be heavy.

1 Beat the egg yolks together with the cold water, coriander and seasoning.

2 Whisk the egg whites until stiff but not dry and gently fold into the egg yolk mixture.

3 Heat the oil in a frying pan, pour in the egg mixture and reduce the heat. Do not stir. Cook until the omelette becomes puffy and golden brown on the underside (carefully lift one edge with a spatula to check).

4 Spoon on the chutney and sprinkle on the Jarlsberg. Fold over and slide onto a warm plate. Eat immediately. (If preferred, before adding the chutney and cheese, place the pan under a hot broiler to set the top.)

Nutty Cheese Balls

An extremely quick and simple recipe. Try making a smaller version to serve as canapés at a drinks party.

Serves 4

INGREDIENTS
1 cup low-fat ricotta cheese
¼ cup Saga blue cheese
1 tbsp finely chopped onion
1 tbsp finely chopped celery stalk
1 tbsp finely chopped parsley
1 tbsp finely chopped gherkin
1 tsp brandy or port (optional)
pinch of paprika
½ cup walnuts or pecans, roughly
   chopped
6 tbsp snipped chives
salt and freshly ground black pepper

Saga blue cheese

celery

gherkins   *ricotta cheese*

onion

walnuts

chives

parsley

paprika

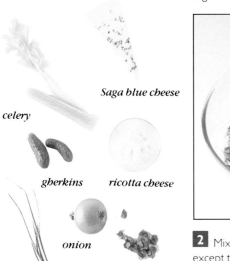

1 Beat the ricotta cheese and Saga blue together using a spoon.

2 Mix in all the remaining ingredients except the snipped chives.

3 Divide the mixture into 12 pieces and roll into balls.

4 Roll each ball gently in the snipped chives. Leave in the fridge to chill for about an hour before serving.

Sweet Potato Roulade

Sweet potato works particularly well as the base for this roulade. Serve in thin slices for a truly impressive dinner party dish.

Serves 6

INGREDIENTS
1 cup low-fat ricotta cheese
5 tbsp low-fat yogurt
6–8 scallions, finely sliced
2 tbsp chopped brazil nuts, roasted
1 lb sweet potatoes, peeled and
   coarsely cubed
12 allspice berries, crushed
4 eggs, separated
¼ cup Edam or Gouda cheese, finely
   grated
salt and freshly ground black pepper
1 tbsp sesame seeds

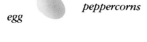

yogurt

sesame seeds

sweet potato

ricotta cheese

Edam

brazil nuts

scallions

peppercorns

egg

1 Preheat the oven to 400°F. Grease and line a 13 × 10 in jelly roll pan with parchment paper, snipping the corners with scissors to fit neatly into the pan.

2 In a small bowl, mix together the ricotta, yogurt, scallions and brazil nuts. Set aside.

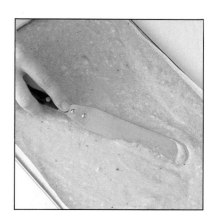

3 Boil or steam the sweet potato until tender. Drain well. Place in a food processor with the allspice and blend until smooth. Spoon into a bowl and stir in the egg yolks and Edam. Season to taste.

4 Whisk the egg whites until stiff but not dry. Fold ⅓ of the egg whites into the sweet potatoes to lighten the mixture before gently folding in the rest.

5 Pour into the prepared pan, tipping it to get the mixture right into the corners. Smooth gently with a spatula and cook in the oven for 10–15 minutes.

COOK'S TIP
Choose the orange-fleshed variety of sweet potato for the most striking color.

6 Meanwhile, lay a large sheet of waxed paper on a clean dish-towel and sprinkle with the sesame seeds. When the roulade is cooked, tip it onto the paper, trim the edges and roll it up. Leave to cool. When cool carefully unroll, spread with the filling and roll up again. Cut into slices to serve.

Ratatouille with Camembert Croûtons

Crisp croûtons and creamy Camembert provide a tasty topping on hot ratatouille. Either buy the ratatouille at a deli counter or make your own.

Serves 2

INGREDIENTS
3 thick slices of white bread
8 oz firm Camembert cheese
4 tbsp olive oil
1 garlic clove, chopped
³/₄–1 lb ratatouille
parsley sprigs, to garnish

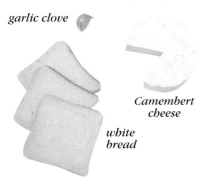
ratatouille

parsley

garlic clove

Camembert cheese

white bread

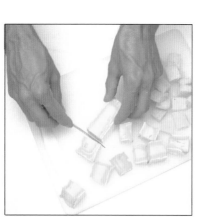

1 Trim the crusts from the bread slices, and discard. Cut the bread and the Camembert into 1 in squares.

2 Heat 3 tbsp of the oil in a frying pan. Add the bread, and cook over a high heat for 5 minutes, stirring constantly, until golden all over. Reduce the heat, add the garlic, and cook for 1 minute more. Remove the croûtons with a slotted spoon.

3 Turn the ratatouille into a pan, and place over a medium heat, stirring occasionally, until hot.

4 Heat the remaining oil in the frying pan. Add the cheese cubes, and sear over a high heat for 1 minute. Divide the hot ratatouille between two serving bowls. Spoon the croûtons and cheese on top, garnish with the parsley, and serve at once.

Omelet aux Fines Herbs

Eggs respond well to fast cooking and combine beautifully with a handful of fresh herbs. Serve with French fries and a green salad.

Serves 1

INGREDIENTS
3 eggs
2 tbsp chopped fresh parsley
2 tbsp chopped fresh chervil
2 tbsp chopped fresh tarragon
1 tbsp chopped fresh chives
1 tbsp butter
salt and freshly ground black pepper
12 oz frozen French fries,
    to serve
4 oz green salad, to serve
1 tomato, to serve

eggs

tarragon

chives

chervil

butter

parsley

1 Break the eggs into a bowl, season to taste and beat with a fork, then add the chopped herbs.

2 Heat an omelet or frying pan over a high heat, add the butter and cook until it foams and browns. Quickly pour in the beaten egg and stir briskly with the back of the fork. When the egg is two-thirds scrambled, let the omelet finish cooking for 10–15 seconds more.

3 Tap the handle of the omelet or frying pan sharply with your fist to make the omelet jump up the sides of the pan, fold and turn onto a plate. Serve with French fries, green salad and a halved tomato.

COOK'S TIP

From start to finish, an omelet should be cooked and on the table in less than a minute. For best results use free-range eggs at room temperature.

Cheese en Croûte with Tomato Sauce

Melt-in-the-mouth cheese sandwiches, pan-fried and served with a tomato sauce.

Serves 4

INGREDIENTS
¼ cup butter, softened
1 small onion, chopped
14 oz can chopped tomatoes
large thyme sprig
8 slices of white bread
4 oz aged Cheddar cheese
2 eggs
2 tbsp milk
2 tbsp peanut oil
salt and freshly ground black pepper
8 Romaine lettuce leaves, to serve

thyme

eggs

chopped tomatoes

onion

milk

Cheddar cheese

butter

white bread

1 Melt 2 tbsp of the butter in a frying pan. Add the onion, and cook for 3–4 minutes until soft.

2 Stir in the chopped tomatoes. Strip the leaves from the thyme sprig, and stir them into the pan. Add salt and pepper to taste. Then cover the pan, and cook for 5 minutes.

3 Meanwhile, spread the remaining butter over the slices of bread.

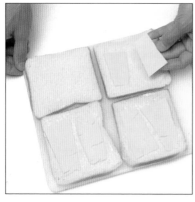

4 Slice the cheese thinly. Arrange on four slices of bread, and sandwich with the remaining slices. Trim the crusts.

5 Beat the eggs and milk together in a bowl. Add salt and pepper to taste, and pour into a shallow dish.

52

6 Heat the oil in a large frying pan. Dip each sandwich in the egg mixture until well-coated. Add to the hot oil, and fry for 2 minutes on each side, until the coating is golden and the cheese has melted. Cut each sandwich into quarters. Arrange on individual plates garnished with the Romaine lettuce leaves. Serve the tomato sauce in a bowl to one side.

COOK'S TIP
If the tomato sauce is a little tart, add a pinch of sugar, or liven it up with a dash of Tabasco.

Sesame Noodle Salad with Hot Peanuts

An orient-inspired salad with crunchy vegetables and a light soy dressing. The hot peanuts make a surprisingly successful union with the cold noodles.

Serves 4

INGREDIENTS

12 oz egg noodles
2 carrots, peeled and cut into fine
    julienne strips
½ cucumber, peeled and cut into
    ½ in cubes
4 oz celeriac, peeled and cut into fine
    julienne strips
6 scallions, finely sliced
8 canned water chestnuts, drained
    and finely sliced
6 oz beansprouts
1 small fresh green chilli, seeded and
    finely chopped
2 tbsp sesame seeds, to serve
1 cup peanuts, to serve

FOR THE DRESSING

1 tbsp dark soy sauce
1 tbsp light soy sauce
1 tbsp honey
1 tbsp rice wine or dry sherry
1 tbsp sesame oil

2 Drain the noodles, refresh in cold water, then drain again.

3 Mix the noodles with all of the prepared vegetables.

1 Preheat the oven to 400°F. Cook the egg noodles in boiling water, following the instructions on the side of the package.

sesame seeds

beansprouts

green chili

scallion

celeriac

cucumber

water chestnuts

peanuts

noodles

carrot

4 Combine the dressing ingredients in a small bowl, then toss into the noodle and vegetable mixture. Divide the salad between 4 plates.

5 Place the sesame seeds and peanuts on separate cookie sheets and place in the oven. Take the sesame seeds out after 5 minutes and continue to cook the peanuts for a further 5 minutes until evenly browned.

6 Sprinkle the sesame seeds and peanuts evenly over each portion and serve at once.

Penne with Eggplant and Mint Pesto

This splendid variation on the classic Italian pesto uses fresh mint rather than basil for a different flavor.

Serves 4

INGREDIENTS
2 large eggplants
salt
1 lb penne
2 oz walnut halves

FOR THE PESTO
1 oz fresh mint
½ oz flat-leaf parsley
1½ oz walnuts
1½ oz Parmesan cheese, finely grated
2 garlic cloves
6 tbsp olive oil
salt and freshly ground black pepper

penne

garlic

walnuts

eggplant

olive oil

parsley

mint

Parmesan

1 Cut the eggplants lengthwise into 1 cm/½ in slices.

2 Cut the slices again crosswise to give short strips.

3 Layer the strips in a colander with salt and leave to stand for 30 minutes over a plate to catch any juices. Rinse well in cool water and drain.

4 Place all the pesto ingredients except the oil in a blender or food processor, blend until smooth, then gradually add the oil in a thin stream until the mixture comes together. Season to taste.

5 Cook the penne following the instructions on the side of the package for about 8 minutes or until nearly cooked. Add the eggplant and cook for a further 3 minutes.

6 Drain well and mix in the mint pesto and walnut halves. Serve immediately.

Campanelle with Yellow Pepper Sauce

Roasted yellow peppers make a deliciously sweet and creamy sauce to serve with pasta.

Serves 4

INGREDIENTS
2 yellow peppers
¼ cup soft goat cheese
½ cup low-fat ricotta cheese
salt and freshly ground black pepper
1 lb short pasta such as campanelle or
  fusilli
¼ cup flaked almonds, toasted,
  to serve

pepper

ricotta cheese

flaked almonds

goat cheese

campanelle

1 Place the whole yellow peppers under a preheated grill until charred and blistered. Place in a paper bag to cool. Peel and remove the seeds.

2 Place the pepper flesh in a blender with the goat cheese and ricotta cheese. Blend until smooth. Season with salt and lots of black pepper.

3 Cook the pasta following the instructions on the side of the package until *al dente*. Drain well.

4 Toss with the sauce and serve sprinkled with the toasted flaked almonds.

Spaghetti with Black Olive and Mushroom Sauce

A rich pungent sauce topped with sweet cherry tomatoes.

Serves 4

INGREDIENTS
1 tbsp olive oil
1 garlic clove, chopped
8 oz mushrooms, chopped
Generous ½ cup black olives, pitted
2 tbsp chopped fresh parsley
1 fresh red chilli, seeded and chopped
1 lb spaghetti
8 oz cherry tomatoes
slivers of Parmesan cheese, to serve
  (optional)

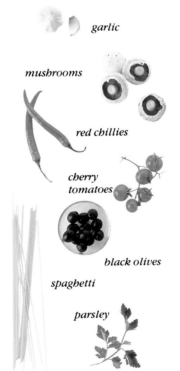

garlic

mushrooms

red chillies

cherry tomatoes

black olives

spaghetti

parsley

1 Heat the oil in a large pan. Add the garlic and cook for 1 minute. Add the mushrooms, cover, and cook over a medium heat for 5 minutes.

2 Place the mushrooms in a blender or food processor with the olives, parsley and red chilli. Blend until smooth.

3 Cook the pasta following the instructions on the side of the package until *al dente*. Drain well and return to the pan. Add the olive mixture and toss together until the pasta is well coated. Cover and keep warm.

4 Heat an ungreased frying pan and shake the cherry tomatoes around until they start to split (about 2–3 minutes). Serve the pasta topped with the tomatoes and garnished with slivers of Parmesan, if desired.

Tagliatelle with Pea Sauce, Asparagus and Broad Beans

A creamy pea sauce makes a wonderful combination with the crunchy young vegetables.

Serves 4

INGREDIENTS
1 tbsp olive oil
1 garlic clove, crushed
6 scallions, sliced
1 cup fresh or frozen baby peas,
    defrosted
12 oz fresh young asparagus
2 tbsp chopped fresh sage, plus extra
    leaves, to garnish
finely grated rind of 2 lemons
1¾ cups fresh vegetable stock or
    water
8 oz fresh or frozen broad beans,
    defrosted
1 lb tagliatelle
4 tbsp low-fat yogurt

lemon

garlic

asparagus

broad beans

peas

yogurt

tagliatelle

sage

scallions

1 Heat the oil in a pan. Add the garlic and scallions and cook gently for 2–3 minutes until softened.

2 Add the peas and ⅓ of the asparagus, together with the sage, lemon rind and stock or water. Bring to a boil, reduce the heat and simmer for 10 minutes until tender. Purée in a blender until smooth.

3 Meanwhile remove the outer skins from the broad beans and discard.

4 Cut the remaining asparagus into 2 in lengths trimming off any tough fibrous stems, and blanch in boiling water for 2 minutes.

5 Cook the tagliatelle following the instructions on the side of the package until *al dente*. Drain well.

COOK'S TIP

Frozen peas and beans have been suggested here to cut down the preparation time, but the dish tastes even better if you use fresh young vegetables when in season.

6 Add the cooked asparagus and shelled beans to the sauce and reheat. Stir in the yogurt and toss into the tagliatelle. Garnish with a few extra sage leaves and serve.

Cilantro Ravioli with Pumpkin Filling

A stunning herb pasta with a superb creamy pumpkin and roast garlic filling.

Serves 4–6

INGREDIENTS
scant cup flour
2 eggs
pinch of salt
3 tbsp chopped fresh cilantro
cilantro sprigs, to garnish

FOR THE FILLING
4 garlic cloves in their skins
1 lb pumpkin, peeled and seeds removed
½ cup ricotta cheese
4 halves sun-dried tomatoes in olive oil, drained and finely chopped, but reserve 2 tbsp of the oil
freshly ground black pepper

cilantro

egg

pumpkin

garlic

flour

ricotta cheese

sun-dried tomatoes

1 Place the flour, eggs, salt and cilantro into a food processor. Pulse until combined.

2 Place the dough on a lightly floured board and knead well for 5 minutes, until smooth. Wrap in plastic wrap and leave to rest in the fridge for 20 minutes.

3 Preheat the oven to 400°F. Place the garlic cloves on a cookie sheet and bake for 10 minutes until softened. Steam the pumpkin for 5–8 minutes until tender and drain well. Peel the garlic cloves and mash into the pumpkin together with the ricotta and drained sun-dried tomatoes. Season with black pepper.

4 Divide the pasta into 4 pieces and flatten slightly. Using a pasta machine, on its thinnest setting, roll out each piece. Leave the sheets of pasta on a clean dish-towel until slightly dried.

5 Using a 3 in crinkle-edged round cutter, stamp out 36 rounds.

6 Top 18 of the rounds with a teaspoonful of mixture, brush the edges with water and place another round of pasta on top. Press firmly around the edges to seal. Bring a large pan of water to a boil, add the ravioli and cook for 3–4 minutes. Drain well and toss into the reserved tomato oil. Serve garnished with cilantro sprigs.

Capellini with Arugula, Snow Peas and Pine Nuts

A light but filling pasta dish with the added pepperiness of fresh arugula.

Serves 4

INGREDIENTS

9 oz capellini or angel-hair pasta
8 oz snow peas
6 oz arugula
¼ cup pine nuts, roasted
2 tbsp Parmesan cheese, finely grated (optional)
2 tbsp olive oil (optional)

arugula

Parmesan

pine nuts

capellini

snow peas

1 Cook the capellini or angel-hair pasta following the instructions on the side of the package until *al dente*.

2 Meanwhile, carefully top and tail the snow peas.

3 As soon as the pasta is cooked, drop in the arugula and snow peas. Drain immediately.

4 Toss the pasta with the roasted pine nuts, and Parmesan and olive oil if using. Serve at once.

COOK'S TIP

Olive oil and Parmesan are optional as they obviously raise the fat content.

Pasta Bows with Fennel and Walnut Sauce

A scrumptious blend of walnuts and crisp steamed fennel.

Serves 4

INGREDIENTS
½ cup walnuts, shelled and roughly chopped
1 garlic clove
1 oz fresh flat-leaf parsley leaves, picked from the stems
½ cup ricotta cheese
1 lb pasta bows
1 lb fennel bulbs
chopped walnuts, to garnish

garlic

pasta bows

ricotta

fennel

parsley

walnut halves

chopped walnuts

I Place the chopped walnuts, garlic and parsley in a food processor. Pulse until roughly chopped. Transfer to a bowl and stir in the ricotta.

2 Cook the pasta following the instructions on the side of the package until *al dente*. Drain well.

3 Slice the fennel thinly and steam for 4–5 minutes until just tender but still crisp.

4 Return the pasta to the pan and add the walnut mixture and the fennel. Toss well and sprinkle with the chopped walnuts. Serve immediately.

Double Tomato Tagliatelle

Sun-dried tomatoes add pungency to this dish, while the broiled fresh tomatoes add bite.

Serves 4

INGREDIENTS
3 tbsp olive oil
1 garlic clove, crushed
1 small onion, chopped
¼ cup dry white wine
6 sun-dried tomatoes, chopped
2 tbsp chopped fresh parsley
½ cup pitted black olives, halved
1 lb fresh tagliatelle
4 tomatoes, halved
Parmesan cheese, to serve
salt and freshly ground black pepper

tomatoes

parsley

garlic clove

sun-dried tomatoes

tagliatelle

dry white wine

onion

black olives

Parmesan cheese

COOK'S TIP

It is essential to buy Parmesan in a piece for this dish. Find a good source – fresh Parmesan should not be unacceptably hard – and shave or grate it yourself. The flavor will be much more intense than that of the pre-grated product.

1 Heat 2 tbsp of the oil in a pan. Add the garlic and onion, and cook for 2–3 minutes, stirring occasionally. Add the wine, sun-dried tomatoes and the parsley. Cook for 2 minutes. Stir in the black olives.

2 Bring a large pan of salted water to a boil. Add the fresh tagliatelle, and cook for 2–3 minutes until just tender. Preheat the broiler.

3 Put the tomatoes on a baking sheet, and brush with the remaining oil. Broil for 3–4 minutes.

4 Drain the pasta, return it to the pan, and toss with the sauce. Serve with the broiled tomatoes, freshly ground black pepper and shavings of Parmesan.

Penne with Fennel, Tomato and Blue Cheese

The anise flavor of the fennel makes it the perfect partner for tomato, especially when topped with blue cheese.

Serves 2

INGREDIENTS
1 fennel bulb
8 oz penne or other dried
  pasta shapes
2 tbsp extra virgin olive oil
1 shallot, finely chopped
1¼ cups strained tomatoes
pinch of sugar
1 tsp chopped fresh oregano
4 oz blue cheese
salt and freshly ground black pepper

fennel bulb

oregano

shallot

penne

strained tomatoes

sugar

blue cheese

1 Cut the fennel bulb in half. Cut away the hard core and root. Slice the fennel thinly, then cut the slices into strips.

2 Bring a large pan of salted water to a boil. Add the pasta, and cook for 10–12 minutes until just tender.

3 Meanwhile, heat the oil in a small saucepan. Add the fennel and shallot, and cook for 2–3 minutes over a high heat, stirring occasionally.

4 Add the tomatoes, sugar and oregano. Cover the pan, and simmer gently for 10–12 minutes, until the fennel is tender. Add salt and pepper to taste. Drain the pasta, and return it to the pan. Toss with the sauce. Serve with blue cheese crumbled over the top.

Lemon and Parmesan Capellini with Herb Bread

Cream is thickened with Parmesan and flavored with lemon to make a superb sauce for pasta.

Serves 2

INGREDIENTS
½ whole wheat stick
¼ cup butter, softened
1 garlic clove, crushed
2 tbsp chopped fresh herbs
8 oz dried or fresh capellini
1 cup light cream
3 oz Parmesan cheese, grated
finely grated rind of 1 lemon
salt and freshly ground black pepper

garlic clove

Parmesan cheese

rosemary

thyme

capellini

butter

lemon

light cream

whole wheat stick *parsley* *oregano*

1 Preheat the oven to 400°F. Cut the whole wheat stick into thick slices.

2 Put the butter in a bowl, and beat with the garlic and herbs. Spread thickly over each slice of bread.

3 Reassemble the stick. Wrap in foil. Support on a baking sheet, and bake for 10 minutes.

4 Meanwhile, bring a large pan of water to a boil, and cook the pasta until just tender. Dried pasta will take 10–12 minutes; fresh pasta will be ready in 2–3 minutes.

5 Pour the cream into another pan, and bring to a boil. Stir in the Parmesan and lemon rind. The sauce should thicken in about 30 seconds.

6 Drain the pasta, return it to the pan, and toss with the sauce. Season to taste, and sprinkle with a little chopped fresh parsley and grated lemon rind, if desired. Serve with the hot herb bread.

Summer Pasta Salad

Tender, young vegetables in a light dressing make a delicious lunch.

Serves 2–3

INGREDIENTS

8 oz fusilli or other dried
  pasta shapes
4 oz baby carrots, trimmed
  and halved
4 oz baby corn, halved lengthwise
2 oz snow peas
4 oz young asparagus spears,
  trimmed
4 scallions, trimmed and shredded
2 tsp white wine vinegar
4 tbsp extra virgin olive oil
1 tbsp whole-grain mustard
salt and freshly ground black pepper

scallions

fusilli

young asparagus

baby carrots

whole-grain mustard

white wine vinegar

baby corn

snow peas

1 Bring a large pan of salted water to a boil. Add the pasta, and cook for about 10–12 minutes, until just tender. Meanwhile, cook the carrots and corn in a second pan of boiling salted water for 5 minutes.

2 Add the snow peas and asparagus spears to the carrots and corn, and cook for 2–3 minutes more. Drain all of the vegetables, and refresh under cold running water. Drain again.

3 Turn the vegetable mixture into a mixing bowl, add the scallions, and toss well together.

4 Drain the pasta, refresh it under cold running water, and drain again. Toss with the vegetables. Mix the vinegar, olive oil and mustard in a jar. Add salt and pepper to taste. Close the jar tightly, and shake well. Pour the dressing over the salad. Toss well, and serve.

Five-spice Vegetable Noodles

Vary this vegetable stir-fry by substituting mushrooms, bamboo shoots, beansprouts, snow peas or water chestnuts for some or all of the vegetables suggested below.

Serves 2–3

INGREDIENTS
8 oz dried egg noodles
2 tbsp sesame oil
2 carrots
1 celery stalk
1 small fennel bulb
2 zucchini, halved and sliced
1 red chili, seeded and chopped
1 in piece of fresh ginger, grated
1 garlic clove, crushed
1½ tsp Chinese five-spice powder
½ tsp ground cinnamon
4 scallions, sliced
¼ cup warm water
1 red chili, seed ed and sliced, to garnish (optional)

carrots *celery stalk* *garlic clove* *fennel bulb* *egg noodles* *zucchini* *five-spice powder* *scallions* *cinnamon* *fresh ginger*

1 Bring a large pan of salted water to a boil. Add the noodles, and cook for 2–3 minutes until just tender. Drain the noodles, return them to the pan, and toss in a little of the oil. Set aside.

2 Cut the carrot and celery into julienne. Cut the fennel bulb in half, and cut out the hard core. Cut into slices. Then cut the slices into julienne.

3 Heat the remaining oil in a wok or frying pan until very hot. Add all the vegetables, including the chili, and stir-fry for 7–8 minutes.

4 Add the ginger and garlic, and stir-fry for 2 minutes. Then add the spices. Cook for 1 minute. Add the scallions. Stir-fry for 1 minute. Pour in the warm water, and cook for 1 minute. Stir in the noodles, and toss well together. Serve sprinkled with sliced red chili, if desired.

Mushroom Bolognese

A quick – and exceedingly tasty – vegetarian version of the classic Italian meat dish.

Serves 4

INGREDIENTS
1 lb mushrooms
1 tbsp olive oil
1 onion, chopped
1 garlic clove, crushed
1 tbsp tomato paste
14 oz can chopped tomatoes
3 tbsp chopped fresh oregano
1 lb fresh pasta
Parmesan cheese, to serve
salt and freshly ground black pepper

mushrooms

chopped tomatoes

oregano

garlic clove

pasta

onion

Parmesan cheese

tomato paste

1 Trim the mushroom stems neatly. Then cut each mushroom into quarters.

2 Heat the oil in a large pan. Add the chopped onion and garlic, and cook for 2–3 minutes.

3 Add the mushrooms to the pan, and cook over a high heat for 3–4 minutes, stirring occasionally.

4 Stir in the tomato paste, chopped tomatoes and 1 tbsp of the oregano. Lower the heat, cover, and cook for about 5 minutes.

5 Meanwhile, bring a large pan of salted water to a boil. Cook the pasta for 2–3 minutes until just tender.

COOK'S TIP
If you prefer to use dried pasta, make this the first thing that you cook. It will take 10–12 minutes, during which time you can make the mushroom mixture. Use 12 oz dried pasta.

6 Season the bolognese sauce with salt and pepper. Drain the pasta, turn it into a bowl, and add the mushroom mixture. Toss to mix well. Serve in individual bowls, topped with shavings of fresh Parmesan and the remaining chopped fresh oregano.

Fried Noodles with Beansprouts and Asparagus

Soft fried noodles contrast beautifully with crisp beansprouts and asparagus.

Serves 2

INGREDIENTS
4 oz dried egg noodles
4 tbsp vegetable oil
1 small onion, chopped
1 in piece of fresh ginger,
  peeled and grated
2 garlic cloves, crushed
6 oz young asparagus spears,
  trimmed
4 oz beansprouts
4 scallions, sliced
3 tbsp soy sauce
salt and freshly ground black pepper

onion

scallions

garlic cloves

fresh ginger

soy sauce

egg noodles

beansprouts

asparagus spears

1 Bring a pan of salted water to a boil. Add the noodles, and cook for 2–3 minutes, until just tender. Drain, and toss in 2 tbsp of the oil.

2 Heat the remaining oil in a wok or frying pan until very hot. Add the onion, ginger and garlic, and stir-fry for 2–3 minutes. Add the asparagus, and stir-fry for 2–3 minutes more.

3 Add the noodles and beansprouts, and stir-fry for 2 minutes.

4 Stir in the scallions and soy sauce. Season to taste, adding salt sparingly as the soy sauce will probably supply enough salt in itself. Stir-fry for 1 minute, then serve at once.

Pasta with Cilantro and Broiled Eggplant

Pasta with a piquant sauce of cilantro and lime – a variation on the classic pesto – is superb served with broiled eggplant.

Serves 2

INGREDIENTS
$^1/_2$ oz cilantro leaves
2 tbsp pine nuts
2 tbsp freshly grated Parmesan cheese
3 garlic cloves
juice of $^1/_2$ lime
7 tbsp olive oil
8 oz dried cellentani or other pasta shapes
1 large eggplant
salt and freshly ground black pepper

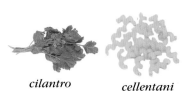
cilantro   *cellentani*

eggplant

pine nuts

Parmesan cheese   *garlic cloves*   *lime*

1 Process the cilantro leaves, pine nuts, Parmesan, garlic, lime juice and 4 tbsp of the olive oil in a food processor or blender for 30 seconds until almost smooth. Bring a large pan of salted water to a boil. Add the pasta, and cook for 10–12 minutes until cooked but still firm to the bite.

2 Meanwhile, cut the eggplant in half lengthwise. Then cut each half into $^1/_4$ in slices. Spread out on a baking sheet, brush with the remaining oil, and season well with salt and black pepper.

3 Broil the eggplant slices for about 4 minutes. Turn them over, and brush with the remaining oil. Season as before. Broil for 4 minutes more.

4 Drain the pasta, turn it into a bowl, and toss with the cilantro sauce. Serve with the broiled eggplant slices.

Spring Vegetable Stir-fry

A colorful, dazzling medley of fresh and sweet young vegetables.

Serves 4

INGREDIENTS
1 tbsp peanut oil
1 garlic clove, sliced
1 in piece of fresh ginger root, finely chopped
4 oz baby carrots
4 oz patty pan squash
4 oz baby corn
4 oz green beans, topped and tailed
4 oz sugar-snap peas, topped and tailed
4 oz young asparagus, cut into 3 in pieces
8 scallions, trimmed and cut into 2 in pieces
4 oz cherry tomatoes

FOR THE DRESSING
juice of 2 limes
1 tbsp honey
1 tbsp soy sauce
1 tsp sesame oil

1 Heat the peanut oil in a wok or large frying pan.

2 Add the garlic and ginger and stir-fry over a high heat for 1 minute.

3 Add the carrots, patty pan squash, baby corn and beans and stir-fry for another 3–4 minutes.

4 Add the sugar-snap peas, asparagus, scallions and cherry tomatoes and stir-fry for a further 1–2 minutes.

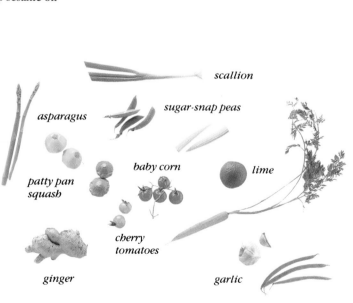

scallion
asparagus
sugar-snap peas
patty pan squash
baby corn
lime
ginger
cherry tomatoes
garlic
green beans

5 Mix the dressing ingredients together and add to the pan.

6 Stir well then cover the pan. Cook for 2–3 minutes more until the vegetables are just tender but still crisp.

COOK'S TIP
Stir-fries take only moments to cook so prepare this dish at the last minute.

Spinach and Potato Galette

Creamy layers of potato, spinach and herbs make a warming supper dish.

Serves 6

INGREDIENTS
2 lb large potatoes
1 lb fresh spinach
2 eggs
14 oz (1¾ cups) low-fat cream
    cheese
1 tbsp grainy mustard
3 tbsp chopped fresh herbs (e.g.
    chives, parsley, chervil or sorrel)
salt and freshly ground black pepper

mustard

parsley

cream cheese

spinach

egg

potatoes

chives

cherry tomatoes

chervil

sorrel

1 Preheat the oven to 350°F. Line a deep 9 in cake pan with parchment paper. Place the potatoes in a large pot and cover with cold water. Bring to a boil and cook for 10 minutes. Drain well and allow to cool slightly before peeling and slicing thinly.

2 Wash the spinach well and place in a large pot with only the water that is clinging to the leaves. Cover and cook, stirring once, until the spinach has just wilted. Drain well in a sieve and squeeze out the excess moisture. Chop finely.

3 Beat the eggs with the cream cheese and mustard then stir in the chopped spinach and fresh herbs.

4 Place a layer of the sliced potatoes in the lined pan, arranging them in concentric circles. Top with a spoonful of the cream cheese mixture and spread out. Continue layering, seasoning with salt and pepper as you go, until all the potatoes and the cream cheese mixture are used up.

5 Cover the pan with a piece of foil and place in a roasting pan.

6 Fill the roasting pan with enough boiling water to come halfway up the sides, and cook in the oven for 45–50 minutes. Turn out onto a plate and serve hot or cold.

COOK'S TIP
Choose firm white or red skinned boiling potatoes for this dish.

Broiled Mixed Peppers with Feta and Green Salsa

Soft, smoky broiled peppers make a lovely combination with the slightly tart salsa.

Serves 4

INGREDIENTS

4 medium peppers in different colors
3 tbsp chopped fresh flat-leaf parsley
3 tbsp chopped fresh dill
3 tbsp chopped fresh mint
½ small red onion, finely chopped
1 tbsp capers, coarsely chopped
¼ cup Greek olives, pitted and sliced
1 fresh green chilli, seeded and finely chopped
4 tbsp pistachios, chopped
5 tbsp extra-virgin olive oil
3 tbsp fresh lime juice
½ cup medium-fat feta cheese, crumbled
1 oz cornichons, finely chopped

olives

feta cheese

green chilli

mint

pistachios

peppers

cornichons

red onion

1 Preheat the broiler. Place the whole peppers on a tray and broil until charred and blistered.

2 Place the peppers in a plastic bag and leave to cool.

COOK'S TIP

Feta cheese is quite salty so if preferred, soak in cold water and drain well before using.

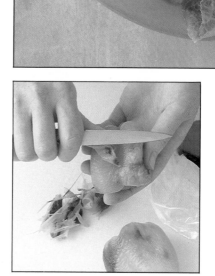

3 Peel, seed and cut the peppers into even strips.

4 Mix all the remaining ingredients together, and stir in the pepper strips.

Beet and Celeriac Gratin

Beautiful ruby-red slices of beets and celeriac make a stunning light accompaniment to any main course dish.

Serves 6

INGREDIENTS
12 oz raw beets
12 oz celeriac
4 thyme sprigs
6 juniper berries, crushed
salt and freshly ground black pepper
½ cup fresh orange juice
½ cup vegetable stock

celeriac

orange juice

juniper berries

beet

thyme

1 Preheat the oven to 375°F. Scrub, peel and slice the beets very finely. Scrub, quarter and peel the celeriac and slice very finely.

2 Fill a 10 in diameter, cast iron, ovenproof or flameproof frying pan with alternate layers of beet and celeriac slices, sprinkling with the thyme, juniper and seasoning between each layer.

3 Mix the orange juice and stock together and pour over the gratin. Place over a medium heat and bring to a boil. Boil for 2 minutes.

4 Cover with foil and place in the oven for 15–20 minutes. Remove the foil and raise the oven temperature to 400°F. Cook for a further 10 minutes until tender and bubbling.

Eggplant, Roast Garlic and Red Pepper Pâté

This is a simple pâté of smoky baked eggplant, sweet pink peppercorns and red peppers, with more than a hint of garlic!

Serves 4

INGREDIENTS
3 medium eggplants
2 red peppers
5 whole garlic cloves
1½ tsp pink peppercorns in brine, drained and crushed
2 tbsp chopped fresh coriander

eggplant

garlic

coriander

pink peppercorns

red pepper

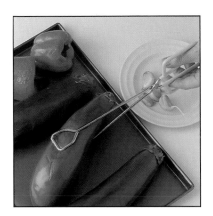

1 Preheat the oven to 400°F. Arrange the whole eggplants, peppers and garlic cloves on a cookie sheet and place in the oven. After 10 minutes remove the garlic cloves and turn over the eggplants and peppers.

2 Peel the garlic cloves and place in the bowl of a blender.

3 After a further 20 minutes remove the blistered and charred peppers from the oven and place in a paper bag. Leave to cool.

4 After a further 10 minutes remove the eggplants from the oven. Split in half and scoop the flesh into a sieve placed over a bowl. Press the flesh with a spoon to remove the bitter juices.

5 Add the mixture to the garlic in the blender and blend until smooth. Place in a large mixing bowl.

6 Peel and chop the red peppers and stir into the eggplant mixture. Mix in the peppercorns and fresh coriander and serve at once.

Zucchini and Asparagus en Papillote

An impressive dinner party accompaniment, these puffed paper parcels should be broken open at the table by each guest, so that the wonderful aroma can be fully appreciated.

Serves 4

INGREDIENTS
2 medium zucchini
1 medium leek
8 oz young asparagus, trimmed
4 tarragon sprigs
4 whole garlic cloves, unpeeled
salt and freshly ground black pepper
1 egg, beaten

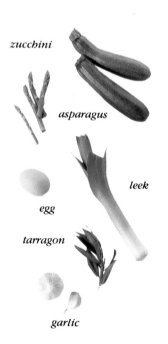

zucchini

asparagus

leek

egg

tarragon

garlic

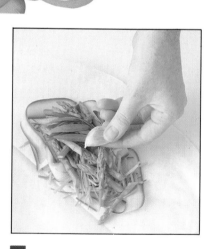

1 Preheat the oven to 400°F. Using a potato peeler slice the zucchini lengthwise into thin strips.

2 Cut the leek into very fine julienne strips and cut the asparagus evenly into 2 in lengths.

3 Cut out 4 sheets of parchment paper 12 × 15 in in size and fold each in half. Draw a large curve to make a heart shape when unfolded. Cut along the inside of the line and open out.

4 Divide the zucchini, asparagus and leek evenly between each paper heart, positioning the filling on one side of the fold line, and topping each with a sprig of tarragon and an unpeeled garlic clove. Season to taste.

COOK'S TIP

Experiment with other vegetables and herbs such as sugar-snap peas and mint or baby carrots and rosemary. The possibilities are endless.

5 Brush the edges lightly with the beaten egg and fold over.

6 Pleat the edges together so that each parcel is completely sealed. Lay the parcels on a cookie sheet and cook for 10 minutes. Serve immediately.

Broccoli and Chestnut Terrine

Served hot or cold, this versatile terrine is equally suitable for a dinner party as for a picnic.

Serves 4–6

INGREDIENTS
1 lb broccoli, cut into small florets
8 oz cooked chestnuts, roughly
    chopped
1 cup fresh wholewheat breadcrumbs
4 tbsp low-fat plain yogurt
2 tbsp Parmesan cheese, finely grated
salt, grated nutmeg and freshly ground
    black pepper
2 eggs, beaten

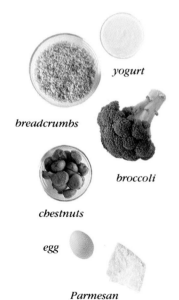

yogurt

breadcrumbs

broccoli

chestnuts

egg

Parmesan

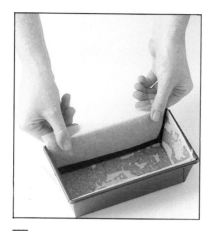

1 Preheat the oven to 350°F. Line a 2 lb loaf pan with a generous layer of parchment paper.

2 Blanch or steam the broccoli for 3–4 minutes until just tender. Drain well. Reserve ¼ of the smallest florets and chop the rest finely.

3 Mix together the chestnuts, breadcrumbs, yogurt and Parmesan, and season to taste.

4 Fold in the chopped broccoli, reserved florets and the beaten eggs.

5 Spoon the broccoli mixture into the prepared pan.

6 Place in a roasting pan and pour in boiling water to come halfway up the sides of the loaf pan. Bake for 20–25 minutes. Remove from the oven and tip out onto a plate or tray. Serve cut into even slices.

Baked Squash

A creamy, sweet and nutty filling makes the perfect topping for tender buttery squash.

Serves 4

INGREDIENTS
2 butternut or acorn squash, 1¼ lb
  each
1 tbsp olive oil
¾ cup canned corn kernels, drained
½ cup unsweetened chestnut purée
5 tbsp low-fat yogurt
salt and freshly ground black pepper
¼ cup fresh goat cheese
snipped chives, to garnish

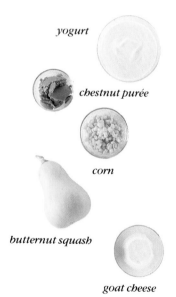

yogurt

chestnut purée

corn

butternut squash

goat cheese

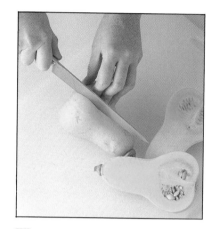

1 Preheat the oven to 350°F. Cut the squash in half lengthwise.

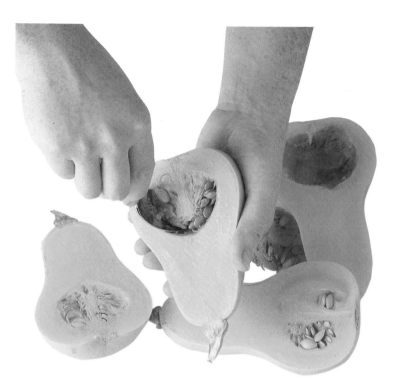

2 Scoop out the seeds with a spoon and discard.

3 Place the squash halves on a cookie sheet and brush the flesh lightly with the oil. Bake in the oven for 30 minutes.

4 Mix together the corn, chestnut purée and yogurt in a bowl. Season to taste.

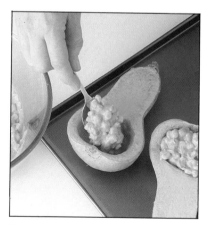

5 Remove the squash from the oven and divide the chestnut mixture between them, spooning it into the hollows.

COOK'S TIP

Use mozzarella or other mild, soft cheeses in place of goat cheese. The cheese can be omitted entirely for a lower-fat alternative.

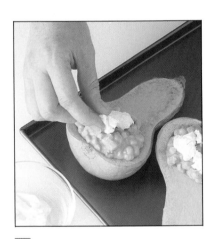

6 Top each half with ¼ of the goat cheese and return to the oven for a further 10–15 minutes. Garnish with snipped chives.

Red Cabbage in Port and Red Wine

A sweet and sour, spicy red cabbage dish, with the added crunch of pears and walnuts.

Serves 6

INGREDIENTS
1 tbsp walnut oil
1 onion, sliced
2 whole star anise
1 tsp ground cinnamon
pinch of ground cloves
1 lb red cabbage, finely shredded
2 tbsp dark brown sugar
3 tbsp red wine vinegar
1¼ cups red wine
⅔ cup port
2 pears, cut into ½ in cubes
½ cup raisins
salt and freshly ground black pepper
½ cup walnut halves

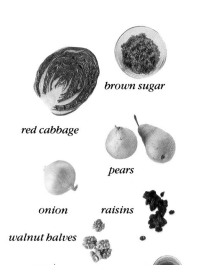

brown sugar

red cabbage

pears

onion   raisins

walnut halves

star anise

port

red wine vinegar

red wine

1 Heat the oil in a large pan. Add the onion and cook gently for about 5 minutes until softened.

2 Add the star anise, cinnamon, cloves and cabbage and cook for about 3 minutes more.

3 Stir in the sugar, vinegar, red wine and port. Cover the pan and simmer gently for 10 minutes, stirring occasionally.

4 Stir in the cubed pears and raisins and cook for a further 10 minutes or until the cabbage is tender. Season to taste. Mix in the walnut halves and serve.

Leek and Caraway Gratin with a Carrot Crust

Tender leeks are mixed with a creamy caraway sauce and a crunchy carrot topping.

Serves 4–6

INGREDIENTS
1 ½ lb leeks, cut into 2 in pieces
⅔ cup fresh vegetable stock or water
3 tbsp dry white wine
1 tsp caraway seeds
pinch of salt
1 ¼ cups skim milk, or as required
2 tbsp butter
¼ cup plain flour

FOR THE TOPPING
2 cups fresh wholewheat
  breadcrumbs
2 cups grated carrot
2 tbsp chopped fresh parsley
3 oz Jarlsberg cheese, coarsely grated
2 tbsp slivered almonds

parsley

vegetable stock

Jarlsberg

leek

breadcrumbs

butter

1 Place the leeks in a large pan. Add the stock or water, wine, caraway seeds and salt. Bring to a simmer, cover and cook for 5–7 minutes until the leeks are just tender.

2 With a slotted spoon, transfer the leeks to an ovenproof dish. Reduce the remaining liquid to half then make the amount up to 1 ½ cups with skim milk.

3 Preheat the oven to 350°F. Melt the butter in a saucepan, stir in the flour and cook without allowing it to color for 1–2 minutes. Gradually add the stock and milk, stirring well after each addition, until you have a smooth sauce. Simmer for 5–6 minutes then pour over the leeks in the dish.

4 Mix all the topping ingredients together in a bowl and sprinkle over the leeks. Bake for 20–25 minutes until golden.

Mushroom and Okra Curry with Fresh Mango Relish

This simple but delicious curry with its fresh gingery mango relish is best served with plain basmati rice.

Serves 4

INGREDIENTS
4 garlic cloves, roughly chopped
1 in piece of fresh ginger root, peeled and roughly chopped
1–2 red chillies, seeded and chopped
¾ cup cold water
1 tbsp sunflower oil
1 tsp coriander seeds
1 tsp cumin seeds
1 tsp ground cumin
2 green cardamom pods, seeds removed and ground
pinch of ground turmeric
1 × 14 oz can chopped tomatoes
1 lb mushrooms, halved or quartered if large
8 oz okra, trimmed and cut into ½ in slices
2 tbsp chopped fresh coriander
basmati rice, to serve

FOR THE MANGO RELISH
1 large ripe mango, about 1¼ lb in weight
1 small garlic clove, crushed
1 onion, finely chopped
2 tsp grated fresh ginger root
1 fresh red chilli, seeded and finely chopped
pinch of salt and sugar

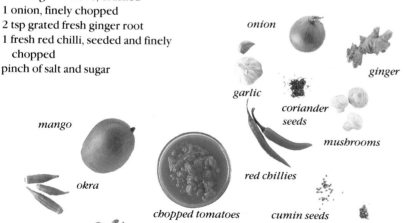

mango
okra
cardamom pods
chopped tomatoes
red chillies
cumin seeds
turmeric
garlic
coriander seeds
onion
ginger
mushrooms

1 For the mango relish, peel the mango and cut off the flesh from the pit.

2 In a bowl mash the mango flesh with a fork or pulse in a food processor, and mix in the rest of the relish ingredients. Set to one side.

3 Place the garlic, ginger, chilli and 3 tbsp of the water into a blender and blend until smooth.

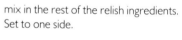

4 Heat the sunflower oil in a large pan. Add the whole coriander and cumin seeds and allow them to sizzle for a few seconds. Add the ground cumin, ground cardamom and turmeric and cook for 1 minute more.

5 Add the paste from the blender, the tomatoes, remaining water, mushrooms and okra. Stir to mix well and bring to a boil. Reduce the heat, cover, and simmer for 5 minutes.

6 Remove the cover, turn up the heat slightly and cook for another 5–10 minutes until the okra is tender. Stir in the fresh coriander and serve with rice and the mango relish.

Potato Gnocchi with Hazelnut Sauce

These delicate potato dumplings are dressed with a creamy hazelnut sauce.

Serves 4

INGREDIENTS
1 ½ lb large potatoes
1 cup plain flour

FOR THE HAZELNUT SAUCE
½ cup skinned, roasted hazelnuts
1 garlic clove, roughly chopped
½ tsp grated lemon rind
½ tsp lemon juice
2 tbsp sunflower oil
scant ¾ cup low-fat ricotta cheese
salt and freshly ground black pepper

lemon

potatoes

flour

hazelnuts

ricotta cheese

garlic

1 Place ⅓ cup of the hazelnuts in a blender with the garlic, grated lemon rind and juice. Blend until coarsely chopped. Gradually add the oil and blend until smooth. Spoon into a bowl and mix in the ricotta cheese. Season to taste.

2 Place the potatoes in a pan of cold water. Bring to the boil and cook for 20–25 minutes. Drain well in a colander.

When cool, peel and purée the potatoes while still warm by passing them through a food mill into a bowl.

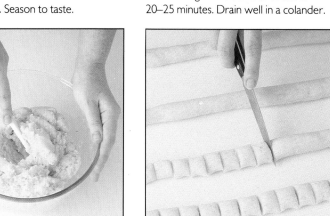

3 Add the flour a little at a time (you may not need all the flour as potatoes vary in texture). Stop adding flour when the mixture is smooth and slightly sticky. Add salt to taste.

4 Roll out the mixture onto a floured board, into a long sausage about ½ in in diameter. Cut into ¾ in lengths.

5 Take 1 piece at a time and press it on to a floured fork. Roll each piece slightly while pressing it along the prongs and off the fork. Flip onto a floured plate or tray. Continue with the rest of the mixture.

COOK'S TIP

A light touch is the key to making soft gnocchi, so handle the dough as little as possible to prevent the mixture from becoming tough.

6 Bring a large pan of water to a boil and drop in 20–25 pieces at a time. They will rise to the surface very quickly. Let them cook for 10–15 seconds more, then lift them out with a slotted spoon. Drop into a dish and keep warm. Continue with the rest of the gnocchi. To heat the sauce, place in a heatproof bowl over a pot of simmering water and heat gently, being careful not to let the sauce curdle. Pour the sauce over the gnocchi. Roughly chop the remaining hazelnuts and scatter over the sauce.

Asparagus Rolls with Herb Butter Sauce

For a taste sensation, try tender asparagus spears wrapped in crisp filo pastry. The buttery herb sauce makes the perfect accompaniment.

Serves 2

INGREDIENTS
4 sheets of filo pastry
1/4 cup butter, melted
16 young asparagus spears, trimmed

FOR THE SAUCE
2 shallots, finely chopped
1 bay leaf
2/3 cup dry white wine
6 oz butter, softened
1 tbsp chopped fresh herbs
salt and freshly ground black pepper
chopped chives, to garnish

fresh herbs

chives

dry white wine

asparagus spears

filo pastry   *butter*

bay leaf   *shallots*

1 Preheat the oven to 400°F. Cut the filo sheets in half. Brush a half sheet with melted butter. Fold one corner of the sheet down to the bottom edge to give a wedge shape.

2 Lay 4 asparagus spears on top at the longest edge, and roll up toward the shortest edge. Using the remaining filo and asparagus spears, make three more rolls in the same way.

3 Lay the rolls on a greased baking sheet. Brush with the remaining melted butter. Bake in the oven for 8 minutes until golden.

4 Meanwhile, put the shallots, bay leaf and wine into a pan. Cover, and cook over a high heat until the wine is reduced to 3–4 tbsp.

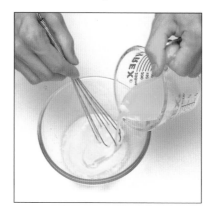

5 Strain the wine mixture into a bowl. Whisk in the butter, a little at a time, until the sauce is smooth and glossy.

6 Stir in the herbs, and add salt and pepper to taste. Return to the pan, and keep the sauce warm. Serve the rolls on individual plates with a salad garnish, if desired. Serve the sauce separately, sprinkled with a few chopped chives.

Tomato Omelet Envelopes

Delicious chive omelet, folded and filled with a
tasty tomato mixture and lots of melting
Camembert cheese.

Serves 2

INGREDIENTS
1 small onion
4 tomatoes
2 tbsp vegetable oil
4 eggs
2 tbsp chopped fresh chives
4 oz Camembert cheese, rind
   removed and diced
salt and freshly ground black pepper

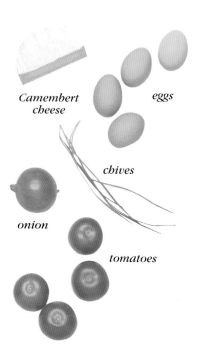

Camembert cheese

eggs

chives

onion

tomatoes

1 Cut the onion in half. Cut each half into thin wedges. Cut the tomatoes into wedges of similar size.

2 Heat 1 tbsp of the oil in a frying pan. Cook the onion for 2 minutes over a moderate heat. Then raise the heat, and add the tomato wedges. Cook for 2 minutes more. Then remove the pan from the heat.

3 Beat the eggs with the chives in a bowl. Add salt and pepper to taste. Heat the remaining oil in an omelet pan. Add half the egg mixture, and tilt the pan to spread thinly. Cook for 1 minute.

4 Flip the omelet over, and cook for 1 minute more. Remove from the pan, and keep hot. Make a second omelet with the remaining egg mixture.

5 Return the tomato mixture to a high heat. Add the cheese, and toss the mixture over the heat for 1 minute.

6 Divide the mixture between the omelets, and fold them over. Serve at once. Add crisp lettuce leaves and chunks of whole wheat bread, if desired.

COOK'S TIP
You may need to wipe the pan clean between the omelets, and reheat a little more oil.

Mushrooms with Leeks and Stilton

Upturned mushrooms make perfect containers for this leek and Stilton filling.

Serves 2–3

INGREDIENTS
1 leek, thinly sliced
6 flat mushrooms
2 garlic cloves, crushed
2 tbsp chopped fresh parsley
1/2 cup butter, softened
4 oz Stilton cheese
freshly ground black pepper
frisée and tomato halves, to garnish

leek

flat mushrooms

butter

parsley

Stilton cheese

garlic cloves

1 Put the leek slices in a small pan with a little water. Cover, and cook for about 5 minutes until tender. Drain. Refresh under cold water, and drain again.

2 Remove the stalks from the flat mushrooms, and set them aside. Put the mushroom caps, hollows uppermost, on an oiled baking sheet.

3 Put the mushroom stalks, garlic and parsley in a food processor or blender. Process for 1 minute. Turn into a bowl. Add the leek and butter, and season with freshly ground black pepper to taste. Preheat the broiler.

4 Crumble the Stilton into the mushroom mixture, and mix well. Divide the Stilton mixture among the mushroom caps, and broil for 6–7 minutes until bubbling. Serve garnished with frisée lettuce and halved tomatoes, if desired.

Tomato and Okra Stew

Okra is an unusual and delicious vegetable. It releases a sticky sap when cooked, which helps to thicken the stew.

Serves 4

INGREDIENTS
1 tbsp olive oil
1 onion, chopped
12 oz jar pimientos, drained
2 x 14 oz cans chopped tomatoes
10 oz okra
2 tbsp chopped fresh parsley
salt and freshly ground black pepper

parsley

chopped tomatoes

onion

pimientos

okra

1 Heat the oil in a pan. Add the onion, and cook for 2–3 minutes.

2 Coarsely chop the pimientos, and add to the onion. Add the chopped tomatoes, and mix well.

3 Cut the tops off the okra, and cut into halves or quarters if large. Add to the tomato sauce in the pan. Season with plenty of salt and pepper.

4 Bring the vegetable stew to a boil. Then lower the heat, cover the pan, and simmer for 12 minutes until the vegetables are tender and the sauce has thickened. Stir in the chopped parsley, and serve at once.

Vegetable Kebabs with Mustard and Honey

A colorful mixture of vegetables and tofu, skewered, glazed and broiled until tender.

Serves 4

INGREDIENTS
1 yellow bell pepper
2 small zucchini
8 oz piece of firm tofu
8 cherry tomatoes
8 button mushrooms
1 tbsp whole-grain mustard
1 tbsp clear honey
2 tbsp olive oil
salt and freshly ground black pepper

TO SERVE
4 portions cooked mixed rice
  and wild rice
lime segments
flat leaf parsley

zucchini

cherry tomatoes

yellow bell pepper

clear honey

whole-grain mustard

button mushrooms

tofu

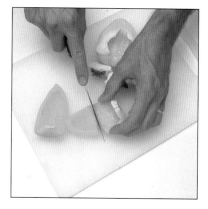

1 Cut the pepper in half, and remove the seeds. Cut each half into quarters, and cut each quarter in half.

2 Remove the ends from the zucchini and peel them decoratively. Then cut each zucchini into eight chunks.

3 Cut the tofu into pieces of a similar size to the vegetables.

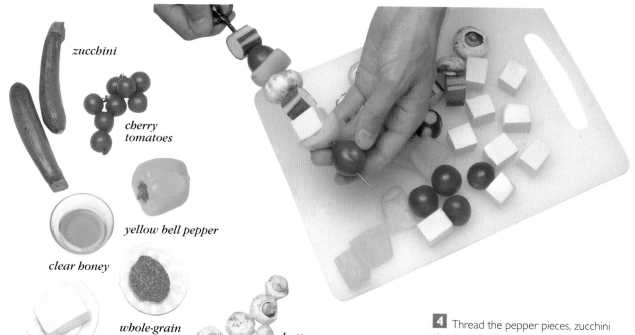

4 Thread the pepper pieces, zucchini chunks, tofu, cherry tomatoes and mushrooms alternately on to four metal or bamboo skewers. Preheat the broiler.

5 Whisk the mustard, honey and olive oil in a small bowl. Add salt and pepper to taste.

6 Put the kebabs on to a baking sheet. Brush with the mustard and honey glaze. Cook under the broiler for 8 minutes, turning once or twice during cooking. Serve with a mixture of long grain and wild rice, and garnish with lime segments and parsley.

COOK'S TIP
If using bamboo skewers, soak them in a bowl of cold water before threading, to prevent them burning when placed under the broiler.

Deep-fried Florets with Tangy Thyme Mayonnaise

Cauliflower and broccoli make a sensational snack when coated in a beer batter and deep-fried. Serve with a tangy mayonnaise.

Serves 2–3

INGREDIENTS
6 oz cauliflower
6 oz broccoli
2 eggs, separated
2 tbsp olive oil
1 cup beer
1¼ cups all-purpose flour
pinch of salt
2 tbsp shredded fresh basil
vegetable oil for deep-frying
²⁄₃ cup good quality mayonnaise
2 tsp chopped fresh thyme
2 tsp grated lemon rind
2 tsp lemon juice
sea salt, for sprinkling

eggs *basil* *all-purpose flour*
mayonnaise *broccoli*
cauliflower *beer*
thyme *lemon*

1 Break the cauliflower and broccoli into small florets, cutting large florets into smaller pieces. Set aside.

2 Beat the egg yolks, olive oil, beer, flour and salt in a bowl. Strain the batter, if necessary, to remove any lumps.

3 Whisk the egg whites until stiff. Fold into the batter with the basil.

4 Heat the oil for deep-frying to 350°F or until a cube of bread, when added to the oil, browns in about 30–45 seconds. Dip the florets in the batter, and deep-fry in batches for 2–3 minutes until the coating is golden and crisp. Drain on paper towels.

5 Mix the mayonnaise, thyme, lemon rind and juice in a small bowl.

6 Sprinkle the florets with sea salt and then serve with the thyme mayonnaise.

Black Bean and Vegetable Stir-fry

The secret of a quick stir-fry is to prepare all the ingredients first. This colorful vegetable mixture is coated in a classic Chinese sauce.

Serves 4

INGREDIENTS
8 scallions
2 cups button mushrooms
1 red bell pepper
1 green bell pepper
2 large carrots
4 tbsp sesame oil
2 garlic cloves, crushed
4 tbsp black bean sauce
6 tbsp warm water
8 oz beansprouts
salt and freshly ground black pepper

scallions

black bean sauce

sesame oil

button mushrooms

red bell pepper

beansprouts

carrots

onion

garlic cloves

green bell pepper

1 Thinly slice the scallions and button mushrooms. Set them to one side in separate bowls.

2 Cut both the bell peppers in half. Remove the seeds, and slice the flesh into thin strips.

3 Cut the carrots in half. Cut each half into thin strips lengthwise. Stack the slices, and cut through them to make very fine strips.

4 Heat the oil in a large wok or frying pan until very hot. Add the scallions and garlic, and stir-fry for 30 seconds.

5 Add the mushrooms, bell peppers and carrots. Stir-fry for 5–6 minutes over a high heat until the vegetables are just beginning to soften.

6 Mix the black bean sauce with the water. Add to the wok or pan, and cook for 3–4 minutes. Stir in the beansprouts, and stir-fry for 1 minute more, until all the vegetables are coated in the sauce. Season to taste. Serve at once.

COOK'S TIP
For best results the oil in the wok must be very hot before adding the vegetables.

Brioche with Mixed Mushrooms

Mushrooms in a rich sherry sauce, served on toasted brioche, make a delectable, light lunch, but would also serve 6 as an appetizer.

Serves 4

INGREDIENTS
6 tbsp butter
1 vegetable bouillon cube
1½ lb shiitake mushrooms, caps only, sliced
8 oz button mushrooms, sliced
3 tbsp dry sherry
1 cup sour cream
2 tsp lemon juice
4 thick slices of brioche
salt and freshly ground black pepper

shiitake and button mushrooms

brioche

butter

bouillon cube

sour cream

lemon

COOK'S TIP

If shiitake mushrooms are too expensive or not available, substitute more button or crimini mushrooms. Always wipe the mushrooms with paper towels before use.

1 Melt the butter in a large pan. Crumble in the bouillon cube, and stir for about 30 seconds.

2 Add the shiitake and button mushrooms to the pan, and cook for 5 minutes over a moderate to high heat, stirring occasionally.

3 Stir in the sherry. Cook for 1 minute, then add the sour cream. Cook, stirring, over a gentle heat for 5 minutes. Stir in the lemon juice, and add salt and pepper to taste. Preheat the broiler.

4 Toast the brioche slices under the broiler until just golden on both sides. Spoon the mushrooms on top, heat briefly under the broiler, and serve. Fresh thyme may be used to garnish, if desired.

Crusty Rolls with Zucchini and Saffron

Split, crusty rolls are filled with zucchini in a creamy tomato sauce flavored with saffron. Use a mixture of green zucchini and yellow summer squash, if possible.

Serves 4

INGREDIENTS
1½ lb small zucchini
1 tbsp olive oil
2 shallots, finely chopped
4 crusty rolls
7 oz can chopped tomatoes
pinch of sugar
a few saffron threads
¼ cup light cream
salt and freshly ground black pepper

zucchini

chopped tomatoes

saffron

shallots

crusty rolls

light cream

1 Preheat the oven to 350°F. Remove the ends from the zucchini, then, using a sharp knife, cut the zucchini into 1½ in lengths. Cut each piece into quarters lengthwise

2 Heat the oil in a large frying pan. Add the shallots, and fry over moderate heat for 1–2 minutes. Put the rolls into the oven to warm through.

3 Add the zucchini to the shallots. Mix well, and cook for 6 minutes, stirring frequently, until just beginning to soften.

4 Stir in the tomatoes and sugar. Steep the saffron threads in a little hot water for a few minutes, then add to the pan with the cream. Cook for 4 minutes, stirring occasionally. Season to taste. Split open the rolls, and fill with the zucchini and sauce.

COOK'S TIP

To avoid heating your oven, heat the rolls in a microwave. Put them on a plate, cover with paper towels, and heat on HIGH for 30–45 seconds.

Potato, Broccoli and Red Bell Pepper Stir-fry

A hot and hearty stir-fry of vegetables with just a hint of fresh ginger.

Serves 2

INGREDIENTS
1 lb potatoes
3 tbsp peanut oil
¼ cup butter
1 small onion, chopped
1 red bell pepper, seeded and chopped
8 oz broccoli, broken into florets
1 in piece of fresh ginger, peeled and grated
salt and freshly ground black pepper

red bell pepper   *butter*

broccoli   *onion*

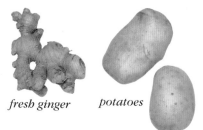

fresh ginger   *potatoes*

COOK'S TIP

Although a wok is the preferred pan for stir-frying, for this recipe, a flat frying pan is best to cook the potatoes quickly.

1 Peel the potatoes, and cut them into ½ in dice.

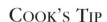

2 Heat the oil in a large frying pan, and add the potatoes. Cook for 8 minutes over a high heat, stirring and tossing occasionally, until the potatoes are browned and just tender.

3 Drain off the oil. Add the butter to the potatoes in the pan. As soon as it melts, add the onion and red bell pepper. Stir-fry for 2 minutes.

4 Add the broccoli florets and ginger to the pan. Stir-fry for 2–3 minutes more, taking care not to break up the potatoes. Add salt and pepper to taste, and serve at once.

Bubble and Squeak with Fried Eggs

Originally made with meat and cabbage in England centuries ago, this dish was named for its noisy cooking.

Serves 2

INGREDIENTS
1/2 Savoy cabbage
1/4 cup butter
1 small onion, finely chopped
1 lb mashed potato
1 tbsp chopped fresh parsley
1 tbsp vegetable oil
2 eggs
salt and freshly ground black pepper
2 tomatoes, halved, to serve

eggs

mashed potato

butter

onion

Savoy cabbage

parsley

1 Cut out and discard the hard core of the cabbage. Strip off and discard the outer layer of leaves. Finely slice the remaining cabbage, and set aside.

2 Melt the butter in a large frying pan. Add the onion, and fry for 2–3 minutes until just tender. Reduce the heat slightly. Add the cabbage, and cook, stirring constantly, for 2–3 minutes.

3 Add the mashed potato to the pan. Stir to combine. Cook for 5–6 minutes until the mixture starts to brown. Stir in the chopped parsley, and add salt and pepper to taste. Transfer the mixture to a serving dish, and keep hot.

4 Wipe the pan clean. Heat the oil, and fry the eggs until just set. Serve the bubble and squeak on individual plates, adding a fried egg and two tomato halves to each portion. Sprinkle with black pepper.

Potato, Spinach and Pine Nut Gratin

Pine nuts add a satisfying crunch to this gratin of wafer-thin potato slices and spinach in a creamy cheese sauce.

Sunday 21 March 2004 - C + G + N
Good + hot. Nice taste + texture.
Next time: more spinach! (baby spinach?)
feta not cheddar to hold up to cooking better
maybe odd milk, not cream?

Serves 2 → 3+

INGREDIENTS
1 lb potatoes   *5 potatoes, unpeeled.*
1 garlic clove, crushed   *2*
3 scallions, thinly sliced   *4 grn onions*
²⁄₃ cup light cream   *half + half*
1 cup milk
8 oz frozen chopped spinach, thawed   *300g*
4 oz Cheddar cheese, grated   *6 oz*
¹⁄₄ cup pine nuts
salt and freshly ground black pepper

spinach

potatoes

garlic clove

pine nuts

scallions

Cheddar cheese

light cream

1 Peel the potatoes, and cut them carefully into wafer-thin slices. Spread them out in a large, heavy-bottomed, nonstick frying pan.

2 Sprinkle the crushed garlic and sliced scallions evenly over the potatoes.

3 Pour the cream and milk over the potatoes. Place the pan over a gentle heat. Cover, and cook for 8 minutes or until the potatoes are tender.

4 Using both hands, squeeze the spinach dry. Add the spinach to the potatoes, mixing lightly. Cover the pan, and cook for 2 minutes more.

5 Add salt and pepper to taste, then spoon the mixture into a shallow casserole. Preheat the broiler.

6 Sprinkle the grated cheese and pine nuts over the spinach mixture. Heat under the broiler for 2–3 minutes until the topping is golden. A simple lettuce and tomato salad makes an excellent accompaniment to this dish.

SALADS

Parmesan and Poached Egg Salad with Croûtons

Soft poached eggs, hot garlic croûtons and cool, crisp salad leaves make an unforgettable combination.

Serves 2

INGREDIENTS
½ small loaf white bread
5 tbsp extra virgin olive oil
2 eggs
4 oz mixed salad leaves
2 garlic cloves, crushed
½ tbsp white wine vinegar
1 oz Parmesan cheese

Parmesan cheese

mixed salad leaves

white bread

garlic cloves

eggs

1 Remove the crust from the bread. Cut the bread into 1 in cubes.

2 Heat 2 tbsp of the oil in a frying pan. Cook the bread for about 5 minutes, tossing the cubes occasionally, until they are golden brown.

3 Meanwhile, bring a pan of water to a boil. Carefully slide in the eggs, one at a time. Gently poach the eggs for 4 minutes until lightly cooked.

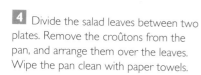

4 Divide the salad leaves between two plates. Remove the croûtons from the pan, and arrange them over the leaves. Wipe the pan clean with paper towels.

5 Heat the remaining oil in the pan, add the garlic and vinegar, and cook over high heat for 1 minute. Pour the warm dressing over each salad.

COOK'S TIP
Add a dash of vinegar to the water before poaching the eggs. This helps to keep the whites together. To make sure that a poached egg has a good shape, swirl the water with a spoon, whirlpool-fashion, before sliding in the egg.

6 Place a poached egg on each salad. Sprinkle with shavings of Parmesan and freshly ground black pepper, if desired.

Classic Greek Salad

If you have ever visited Greece, you'll know that a Greek salad with a chunk of bread makes a delicious, filling meal.

Serves 4

INGREDIENTS
1 Romaine lettuce
$^1/_2$ cucumber, halved lengthwise
4 tomatoes
8 scallions
$^1/_3$ cup Greek black olives
4 oz feta cheese
6 tbsp white wine vinegar
$^1/_2$ cup extra virgin olive oil
salt and freshly ground black pepper

Romaine lettuce

tomatoes

feta cheese

black olives

white wine vinegar

cucumber

scallions

COOK'S TIP
The salad can be assembled in advance and chilled, but add the lettuce and dressing just before serving. Keep the dressing at room temperature as chilling deadens its flavor.

1 Tear the lettuce leaves into pieces, and place them in a large mixing bowl. Slice the cucumber, and add to the bowl.

2 Cut the tomatoes into wedges, and put them into the bowl.

3 Slice the scallions. Add them to the bowl with the olives, and toss well.

4 Cut the feta cheese into cubes, and add to the salad.

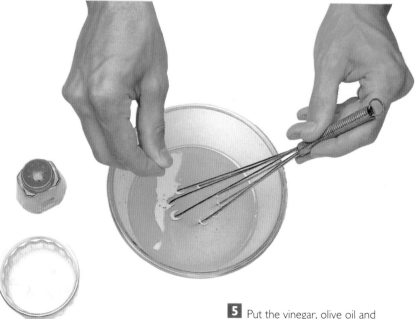

5 Put the vinegar, olive oil and seasoning into a small bowl, and whisk well. Pour the dressing over the salad, and toss to combine. Serve at once, with olives and chunks of bread, if desired.

Belgian Endive, Fruit and Nut Salad

Mildly bitter endive is wonderful with sweet fruit, and is especially delicious when complemented by a creamy curry sauce.

Serves 4

INGREDIENTS

3 tbsp mayonnaise
1 tbsp strained, plain yogurt
1 tbsp mild curry paste
6 tbsp light cream
$1/2$ iceberg lettuce
2 heads of Belgian endive
$1/2$ cup cashews
$1^{1}/_{4}$ cups flaked coconut
2 red apples
$1/2$ cup currants

currants

iceberg lettuce

curry paste

mayonnaise

cashews

red apples

light cream

flaked coconut

Belgian endive

1 Mix the mayonnaise, yogurt, curry paste and light cream in a small bowl. Cover, and chill until required.

2 Tear the iceberg lettuce into pieces, and put into a salad bowl.

3 Cut the root end off each head of Belgian endive, and discard. Slice the endive, and add it to the salad bowl.

4 Preheat the broiler. Toast the cashews for 2 minutes until they are golden. Turn into a bowl, and set aside. Spread out the coconut flakes on a baking sheet. Broil for 1 minute.

5 Quarter the apples, and cut out the cores. Slice the apples, and add to the lettuce with the cashews, flaked coconut, and currants.

COOK'S TIP
Watch the coconut and cashews very carefully when broiling, as they brown very fast.

6 Spoon the dressing over the salad. Toss lightly, and serve.

Broiled Bell Pepper Salad

Broiled bell peppers are delicious served hot with a sharp dressing. You can also eat them cold.

Serves 2

INGREDIENTS
1 red bell pepper
1 green bell pepper
1 yellow or orange bell pepper
$\frac{1}{2}$ radicchio, separated into leaves
$\frac{1}{2}$ frisée, separated into leaves
1$\frac{1}{2}$ tsp white wine vinegar
2 tbsp extra virgin olive oil
6 oz goat cheese
salt and freshly ground black pepper

frisée

green bell pepper

red bell pepper

yellow bell pepper

goat cheese

white wine vinegar

radicchio

1 Preheat the broiler. Cut all the bell peppers in half. Cut each half into pieces.

2 Put the pepper pieces on a rack set over a broiler pan. Broil for 10 minutes.

3 Meanwhile, divide the radicchio and frisée leaves between two plates. Chill until required.

4 Mix the vinegar and olive oil in a jar. Add salt and pepper to taste. Close the jar tightly, and shake well.

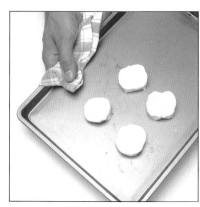
5 Slice the goat cheese, and place on a baking sheet. Broil for 1 minute.

6 Arrange the peppers and broiled goat cheese on the salads. Pour over the dressing, and grind a little extra black pepper over each.

COOK'S TIP
Broil the bell peppers until they just start to blacken around the edges – don't let them burn.

Zucchini, Carrots and Pecans in Pita Bread

Chunks of fried zucchini served with a tangy salad in pita pockets.

Serves 2

INGREDIENTS
2 carrots
¼ cup pecan nuts
4 scallions, sliced
¼ cup strained, plain yogurt
7 tsp olive oil
1 tsp lemon juice
1 tbsp chopped fresh mint
2 zucchini
¼ cup all-purpose flour
2 pita breads
salt and freshly ground black pepper
shredded lettuce, to serve

zucchini

scallions

pecan nuts   *lemon*

mint

strained, plain yogurt

carrots

1 Remove the ends from the carrots. Grate them coarsely into a bowl.

2 Stir in the pecans and scallions, and toss well together.

3 In a clean bowl, whisk the yogurt with 1½ tsp of the olive oil, the lemon juice and the fresh mint. Stir the dressing into the carrot mixture, and mix well. Cover, and chill until required.

4 Remove the ends from the zucchini. Cut them diagonally into slices. Season the flour with salt and pepper. Spread it on a plate, and coat the zucchini slices.

COOK'S TIP
Do not fill the pita breads too soon or the carrot mixture will make the bread soggy.

5 Heat the remaining oil in a large frying pan. Add the coated zucchini slices, and cook for 3–4 minutes, turning once, until browned. Drain the zucchini on paper towels.

6 Make a slit in each pita bread to form a pocket. Fill the pitas with the carrot mixture and the zucchini slices. Serve on a bed of shredded lettuce.

Zucchini Puffs with Salad and Balsamic Dressing

This unusual salad consists of deep-fried zucchini, flavored with mint, and served warm on a bed of salad leaves with a balsamic dressing.

Serves 2

INGREDIENTS
1 lb zucchini
1½ cups fresh white bread crumbs
1 egg
pinch of cayenne pepper
1 tbsp chopped fresh mint
oil for deep-frying
3 tbsp balsamic vinegar
3 tbsp extra virgin olive oil
7 oz mixed salad leaves
salt and freshly ground black pepper

zucchini

white bread crumbs

balsamic vinegar

egg

mint

mixed salad leaves

1 Remove the ends from the zucchini. Coarsely grate them, and put into a colander. Squeeze out the excess water. Then put the zucchini into a bowl.

2 Add the bread crumbs, egg, cayenne, mint and seasoning. Mix well.

3 Shape the zucchini mixture into balls, about the size of walnuts.

4 Heat the oil for deep-frying to 350°F or until a cube of bread, when added to the oil, browns in 30–40 seconds. Deep-fry the zucchini balls in batches for 2–3 minutes. Drain on paper towels.

5 Whisk the vinegar and oil together, and season well.

6 Put the salad leaves in a bowl, and pour over the dressing. Add the zucchini puffs, and toss lightly together. Serve at once, while the puffs are still crisp.

Vegetable and Satay Salad

Baby new potatoes, tender vegetables and crunchy chick-peas are smothered in a creamy peanut dressing.

Serves 4

INGREDIENTS
1 lb baby new potatoes
1 small head cauliflower, broken
  into small florets
8 oz green beans, trimmed
14 oz can chick-peas, drained
4 oz watercress sprigs
4 oz beansprouts
8 scallions, sliced
4 tbsp crunchy peanut butter
$^2/_3$ cup hot water
1 tsp chili sauce
2 tsp brown sugar
1 tsp soy sauce
1 tsp lime juice

cauliflower

watercress

soy sauce

scallions

crunchy peanut butter

brown sugar

chick-peas

beansprouts

chili sauce

lime

green beans

baby new potatoes

1 Put the potatoes into a pan, and add water just to cover. Bring to a boil, and cook for 10–12 minutes or until the potatoes are just tender when pierced with the point of a sharp knife. Drain, and refresh under cold running water. Drain once again.

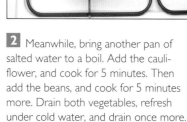

2 Meanwhile, bring another pan of salted water to a boil. Add the cauliflower, and cook for 5 minutes. Then add the beans, and cook for 5 minutes more. Drain both vegetables, refresh under cold water, and drain once more.

3 Put the cauliflower and beans into a large bowl, and add the chick-peas. Halve the potatoes, and add. Toss lightly. Mix the watercress, beansprouts and scallions together. Divide among four plates, and pile the vegetables on top.

4 Put the peanut butter into a bowl, and stir in the water. Add the chili sauce, brown sugar, soy sauce and lime juice. Whisk well, then drizzle the dressing over the vegetables.

Fresh Spinach and Avocado Salad

Young, tender spinach leaves make a change from lettuce and are delicious served with avocado, cherry tomatoes and radishes in a tofu sauce.

Serves 2–3

INGREDIENTS
1 large avocado
juice of 1 lime
8 oz fresh baby spinach leaves
4 oz cherry tomatoes
4 scallions, sliced
$\frac{1}{2}$ cucumber
2 oz radishes, sliced

FOR THE DRESSING
4 oz soft silken tofu
3 tbsp milk
2 tsp prepared mustard
$\frac{1}{2}$ tsp white wine vinegar
pinch of cayenne
salt and freshly ground black pepper

tofu   scallions

spinach leaves

cherry tomatoes

avocado

white wine vinegar

mustard

lime

cayenne

cucumber

radishes

milk

1 Cut the avocado in half, remove the pit, and strip off the skin. Cut the flesh into slices. Transfer to a plate, drizzle over the lime juice, and set aside.

2 Wash and dry the spinach leaves. Put them in a mixing bowl.

COOK'S TIP
Use soft silken tofu rather than the block variety. It can be found in most supermarkets in the vegetable or refrigerated sections.

3 Cut the larger cherry tomatoes in half, and add all the tomatoes to the mixing bowl, with the scallions. Cut the cucumber into chunks, and add to the bowl with the sliced radishes.

4 Make the dressing. Put the tofu, milk, mustard, wine vinegar and cayenne in a food processor or blender. Add salt and pepper to taste. Process for 30 seconds until smooth. Scrape the dressing into a bowl, and add a little extra milk if you like a thinner dressing. Sprinkle with a little extra cayenne, and garnish with radish roses and herb sprigs, if desired.

New Spring Salad

This chunky salad makes a satisfying meal. Use other spring vegetables, if you like.

Serves 4

INGREDIENTS

1½ lb small new potatoes, halved
14 oz can fava beans, drained
4 oz cherry tomatoes
½ cup walnut halves
2 tbsp white wine vinegar
1 tbsp whole-grain mustard
4 tbsp olive oil
pinch of sugar
8 oz young asparagus spears,
  trimmed
6 scallions, trimmed
salt and freshly ground black pepper
baby spinach leaves, to serve

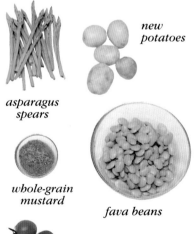

asparagus spears

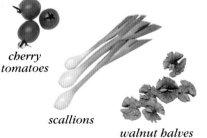

new potatoes

whole-grain mustard

fava beans

cherry tomatoes

scallions

walnut halves

1 Put the potatoes in a pan. Cover with cold water, and bring to a boil. Cook for 10 – 12 minutes, until tender. Meanwhile, turn the fava beans into a bowl. Cut the tomatoes in half, and add them to the bowl with the walnuts.

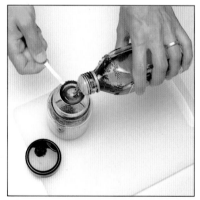

2 Put the white wine vinegar, mustard, olive oil and sugar into a jar. Add salt and pepper to taste. Close the jar tightly, and shake well.

3 Add the asparagus to the potatoes, and cook for 3 minutes more. Drain the cooked vegetables well. Cool under cold running water, and drain again. Thickly slice the potatoes, and cut the scallions into halves.

4 Add the asparagus, potatoes and scallions to the bowl containing the fava bean mixture. Pour the dressing over the salad, and toss well. Serve on a bed of baby spinach leaves.

Potato Salad with Egg and Lemon Dressing

Potato salads are a popular addition to any salad spread and are enjoyed with an assortment of cold meats and fish. This recipe draws on the contrasting flavors of egg and lemon. Chopped parsley provides a fresh finish.

Serves 4

INGREDIENTS
2 lb new potatoes, scrubbed or scraped
salt and pepper
1 medium onion, finely chopped
1 egg, hard-cooked
1¼ cups mayonnaise
1 clove garlic, crushed
finely grated zest and juice of 1 lemon
4 tbsp chopped fresh parsley

COOK'S TIP
At certain times of the year potatoes are inclined to fall apart when boiled. This usually coincides with the end of a particular season when potatoes become starchy. Early-season varieties are therefore best for making salads.

egg

garlic

onion

lemon

new potatoes

1 Bring the potatoes to a boil in a saucepan of salted water. Simmer for 20 minutes. Drain and allow to cool. Cut the potatoes into large dice, season well, and combine with the onion.

2 Shell the hard-cooked egg and grate into a mixing bowl, then add the mayonnaise. Combine the garlic and lemon zest and juice in a small bowl and stir into the mayonnaise.

3 Fold in the chopped parsley, mix thoroughly into the potatoes, and serve.

Leeks with Parsley, Egg, and Walnut Dressing

In French cooking, leeks are valued for their smooth texture as well as their flavor. They make a wonderful salad, which should be eaten slightly warm, so it is the ideal dish to serve with assorted pâtés and boiled new potatoes for a gourmet picnic feast.

Serves 4

INGREDIENTS
1½ lb young leeks
1 egg

DRESSING
1 oz fresh parsley
2 tbsp olive oil, preferably French
juice of ½ lemon
½ cup broken walnuts, toasted
1 tsp superfine sugar
salt and pepper

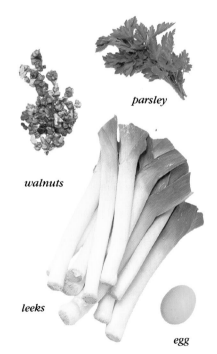
parsley

walnuts

leeks

egg

1 Bring a saucepan of salted water to a boil. Cut the leeks into 4 in lengths and rinse well to flush out any grit or soil. Cook the leeks for 8 minutes. Drain and part-cool under running water.

2 Lower the egg into boiling water and cook for 12 minutes. Cool under running water, shell, and set aside.

3 For the dressing, finely chop the parsley in a food processor.

4 Add the olive oil, lemon juice, and toasted walnuts. Blend for 1–2 minutes until smooth.

5 Adjust the consistency with about ⅓ cup water. Add the sugar and season to taste with salt and pepper.

6 Place the leeks on an attractive plate, then spoon on the sauce. Finely grate the hard-cooked egg and scatter over the sauce. Serve at room temperature.

Deep-fried Zucchini with Chili Sauce

Crunchy coated zucchini are great served with a fiery tomato sauce.

Serves 2

INGREDIENTS
1 tbsp olive oil
1 onion, finely chopped
1 red chili, seeded and finely diced
2 tsp hot chili powder
14 oz can chopped tomatoes
1 vegetable bouillon cube
$^1/_4$ cup hot water
1 lb zucchini
$^2/_3$ cup milk
$^1/_2$ cup all-purpose flour
oil for deep-frying
salt and freshly ground black pepper

TO SERVE
lettuce leaves
watercress sprigs
slices of seeded bread
thyme sprigs, to garnish

zucchini

chopped tomatoes

onion

red chili

all-purpose flour

bouillon cube

milk

chili powder

3 Meanwhile, remove the ends from the zucchini. Cut them into $^1/_4$ in slices.

5 Heat the oil for deep-frying to 350°F or until a cube of bread, when added to the oil, browns in 30–45 seconds. Add the zucchini slices in batches, and deep-fry for 3–4 minutes until crisp. Drain on paper towels.

6 Place two or three lettuce leaves on each serving plate. Add a few sprigs of watercress, and fan out the bread slices to one side. Season the sauce, spoon some on to each plate, top with the zucchini and garnish with the sprigs of thyme. Serve at once with a crisp salad and bread.

1 Heat the oil in a pan. Add the onion, and cook for 2–3 minutes. Add the chili. Stir in the chili powder, and cook for 30 seconds.

2 Add the tomatoes. Crumble in the bouillon cube, and stir in the water. Cover and cook for 10 minutes.

4 Pour the milk into one shallow dish, and spread out the flour in another. Dip the zucchini first in the milk, then into the flour, until well-coated.

Cumin-spiced Large Zucchini and Spinach

A great way to enjoy the giant zucchini that escaped in the garden is with spinach and cream.

Serves 2

INGREDIENTS
1 lb zucchini
2 tbsp vegetable oil
2 tsp cumin seeds
1 small red chili, seeded and
  finely chopped
2 tbsp water
2 oz tender, young spinach leaves
6 tbsp light cream
salt and freshly ground black pepper

spinach leaves

cumin seeds

large zucchini

light cream

red chili

1 Peel the zucchini, and cut it in half. Scoop out the seeds. Cut the flesh into ¹/₂ in cubes.

2 Heat the oil in a large frying pan. Add the cumin seeds and the chopped chili. Cook for 1 minute.

3 Add the zucchini and water to the pan. Cover with foil or a lid, and simmer for 8 minutes, stirring occasionally, until the zucchini is just tender. Remove the cover, and cook for 2 minutes more or until most of the water has evaporated.

4 Put the spinach leaves in a colander. Rinse well under cold water, drain and pat dry with paper towels. Tear into rough pieces.

5 Add the spinach to the zucchini. Replace the cover, and cook gently for 1 minute.

6 Stir in the cream, and cook over a high heat for 2 minutes. Add salt and pepper to taste, and serve. An Indian rice dish would be a good accompaniment. As an alternative, serve with naan bread.

Chili Beans with Basmati Rice

Red kidney beans, tomatoes and chili make a great combination. Serve with pasta or pita bread instead of rice, if you prefer.

Serves 4

INGREDIENTS
2 cups basmati rice
2 tbsp olive oil
1 large onion, chopped
1 garlic clove, crushed
1 tbsp hot chili powder
1 tbsp all-purpose flour
1 tbsp tomato paste
14 oz can chopped tomatoes
14 oz can red kidney beans, drained
²/₃ cup hot vegetable stock
chopped fresh parsley, to garnish
salt and freshly ground black pepper

basmati rice

chopped tomatoes

chili powder

onion

tomato paste

garlic clove

stock cube

red kidney beans

all-purpose flour

1 Wash the rice several times under cold running water. Drain well. Bring a large pan of water to a boil. Add the rice, and cook for 10–12 minutes, until tender. Meanwhile, heat the oil in a frying pan. Add the onion and garlic, and cook for 2 minutes.

2 Stir the chili powder and flour into the onion and garlic mixture. Cook for 2 minutes, stirring frequently.

3 Stir in the tomato paste and chopped tomatoes. Rinse the kidney beans under cold water, drain well, and add to the pan with the hot vegetable stock. Cover and cook for 12 minutes, stirring occasionally.

4 Season the chili sauce with salt and pepper. Drain the rice, and serve at once, with the chili beans, sprinkled with a little chopped fresh parsley.

Spicy Cauliflower and Potato Salad

A delicious, cold vegetable salad with a hot and spicy dressing.

Serves 2–3

INGREDIENTS
1 cauliflower
2 potatoes
1½ tsp caraway seeds
1 tsp ground coriander
½ tsp hot chili powder
juice of 1 lemon
4 tbsp olive oil
salt and freshly ground black pepper

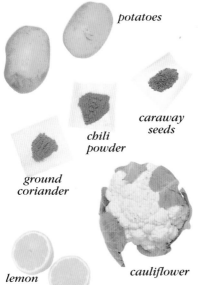

potatoes

caraway seeds

chili powder

ground coriander

lemon

cauliflower

1 Break the cauliflower into small florets. Peel the potatoes, and cut them into chunks.

2 Bring a large pan of water to a boil. Add the cauliflower florets and potato chunks, and cook for 8 minutes until they are just tender.

3 Meanwhile, heat a nonstick frying pan. Add the caraway seeds, and fry, shaking the pan constantly, for 1 minute. Turn the roasted seeds into a bowl, and add the ground coriander and chili powder, with salt and pepper to taste. Stir in the lemon juice and olive oil. Mix to a paste.

4 Drain the vegetables well. Add them to the bowl, and toss to coat in the chili dressing. Serve at once, with hot pita bread or brown rice.

Bengali-style Vegetables

A hot, dry curry using spices that do not require long, slow cooking.

Serves 4

INGREDIENTS

½ cauliflower, broken into
  small florets
1 large potato, peeled and cut into
  1 in dice
4 oz green beans, trimmed
2 zucchini, halved lengthwise
  and sliced
2 green chilies
1 in piece of fresh ginger, peeled
½ cup plain yogurt
2 tsp ground coriander
½ tsp ground turmeric
2 tbsp ghee or vegetable oil
½ tsp garam masala
1 tsp cumin seeds
2 tsp sugar
pinch each of ground cloves,
  ground cinnamon and
    ground cardamom
salt and freshly ground black pepper

1 Bring a large pan of water to a boil. Add the cauliflower and potato, and cook for 5 minutes. Add the beans and zucchini, and cook for 2–3 minutes.

2 Meanwhile, cut the chilies in half, remove the seeds, and coarsely chop the flesh. Finely chop the ginger. Mix the chilies and ginger in a small bowl.

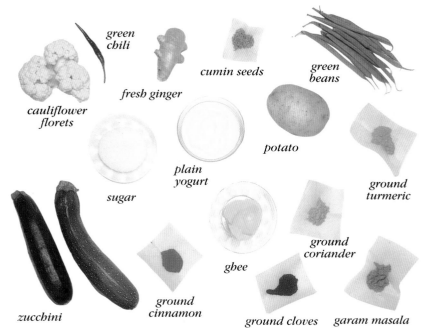

green
chili

cumin seeds

green
beans

fresh ginger

cauliflower
florets

potato

plain
yogurt

ground
turmeric

sugar

ground
coriander

ghee

zucchini

ground
cinnamon

ground cloves

garam masala

3 Drain the vegetables, and turn them into a bowl. Add the chili and ginger mixture, with the yogurt, ground coriander and turmeric. Season with plenty of salt and pepper, and mix well.

4 Heat the ghee or oil in a large frying pan. Add the vegetable mixture, and cook over a high heat for 2 minutes, stirring from time to time.

5 Stir in the garam masala and cumin seeds, and cook for 2 minutes.

6 Stir in the sugar and remaining spices, and cook for 1 minute or until all the liquid has evaporated.

COOK'S TIP

If ghee is not available, you can clarify your own butter. Melt ¼ cup butter slowly in a small pan. Remove from the heat, and leave for about 5 minutes. Then pour off the clear yellow clarified butter, leaving the sediment in the pan.

Vegetable Fajita

A colorful medley of mushrooms and bell peppers in a spicy sauce, wrapped in tortillas and served with creamy guacamole.

Serves 2

INGREDIENTS
1 onion
1 red bell pepper
1 green bell pepper
1 yellow bell pepper
1 garlic clove, crushed
8 oz mushrooms
6 tbsp vegetable oil
2 tbsp medium chili powder
salt and freshly ground black pepper

FOR THE GUACAMOLE
1 ripe avocado
1 shallot, coarsely chopped
1 green chili, seeded and
  coarsely chopped
juice of 1 lime

TO SERVE
4–6 flour tortillas, warmed
1 lime, cut into wedges
cilantro sprigs

green bell pepper

yellow bell pepper

red bell pepper

mushrooms

avocado

green chili

shallot

garlic clove

lime

chili powder

onion

1 Slice the onion. Cut the bell peppers in half, remove the seeds, and cut the flesh into strips. Combine the onion and peppers in a bowl. Add the crushed garlic, and mix lightly.

2 Remove the mushroom stalks. Save for making stock, or discard. Slice the mushroom caps, and add to the pepper mixture in the bowl. Mix the oil and chili powder in a cup, pour over the vegetable mixture, and stir well. Set aside.

3 Make the guacamole. Cut the avocado in half, and remove the pit and the peel. Put the flesh into a food processor or blender with the shallot, green chili and lime juice. Process for 1 minute until smooth. Scrape into a small bowl, cover tightly, and put in the fridge to chill until required.

4 Heat a frying pan or wok until very hot. Add the marinated vegetables, and stir-fry over a high heat for 5–6 minutes until the mushrooms and pepper are just tender. Season well. Spoon a little of the filling on to each tortilla, and roll up. Garnish with fresh cilantro, and serve with the guacamole and lime wedges.

Curried Eggs

Hard-boiled eggs are served on a bed of mild, creamy sauce with a hint of curry.

Serves 2

INGREDIENTS

4 eggs
1 tbsp sunflower oil
1 small onion, finely chopped
1 in piece of fresh ginger,
  peeled and grated
$^1\!/_2$ tsp ground cumin
$^1\!/_2$ tsp garam masala
$1^1\!/_2$ tbsp tomato paste
2 tsp tandoori paste
2 tsp lemon juice
$^1\!/_4$ cup light cream
1 tbsp chopped fresh cilantro
salt and freshly ground black pepper
cilantro sprigs, to garnish

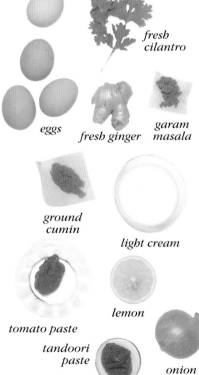

eggs

fresh cilantro

fresh ginger

garam masala

ground cumin

light cream

tomato paste

lemon

tandoori paste

onion

1 Put the eggs in a pan of water. Bring to a boil, lower the heat, and simmer for 10 minutes.

2 Meanwhile, heat the oil in a frying pan. Cook the onion for 2–3 minutes. Add the ginger, and cook for 1 minute.

3 Stir in the ground cumin, garam masala, tomato paste, tandoori paste, lemon juice and cream. Cook for 1–2 minutes, then stir in the cilantro. Add salt and pepper to taste.

4 Drain the eggs, remove the shells, and cut each egg in half. Spoon the sauce into a serving bowl, top with the eggs, and garnish with the cilantro sprigs. Serve at once.

Breaded Eggplant with Hot Vinaigrette

Crisp on the outside, beautifully tender within, these eggplant slices taste wonderful with a spicy dressing flavored with chili and capers.

Serves 2

INGREDIENTS
1 large eggplant
$\frac{1}{2}$ cup all-purpose flour
2 eggs, beaten
2 cups fresh white bread crumbs
vegetable oil for frying
1 head radicchio
salt and freshly ground black pepper

FOR THE DRESSING
2 tbsp olive oil
1 garlic clove, crushed
1 tbsp capers, drained
1 tbsp white wine vinegar
1 tbsp chili oil

COOK'S TIP
When serving a salad with a warm dressing, use robust leaves that will stand up to the heat.

1 Remove the ends from the eggplant. Cut it into $\frac{1}{4}$ in slices. Set aside.

2 Season the flour with a generous amount of salt and black pepper. Spread out in a shallow dish. Pour the beaten eggs into a second dish. Spread out the bread crumbs in a third.

3 Dip the eggplant slices in the flour, then in the beaten egg and finally in the bread crumbs, patting them on to make an even coating.

eggplant
bread crumbs
all-purpose flour
eggs
radicchio
capers
white wine vinegar
garlic clove

4 Pour vegetable oil into a large frying pan to a depth of about $\frac{1}{4}$ in. Heat the oil, then fry the eggplant slices for 3–4 minutes, turning once. Drain well on paper towels.

5 Heat the olive oil in a small pan. Add the garlic and the capers, and cook over gentle heat for 1 minute. Increase the heat, add the vinegar, and cook for 30 seconds. Stir in the chili oil, and remove the pan from the heat.

6 Arrange the radicchio leaves on two plates. Top with the hot eggplant slices. Drizzle over the vinaigrette, and serve.

Creamy Cannellini Beans with Asparagus

Cannellini beans in a creamy sauce contrast with tender asparagus in this tasty toast topper.

Serves 2

INGREDIENTS
2 tsp butter
1 small onion, finely chopped
1 small carrot, grated
1 tsp fresh thyme leaves
14 oz can cannellini beans, drained
²/₃ cup light cream
4 oz young asparagus spears, trimmed
2 slices of fresh sliced whole wheat bread
salt and freshly ground black pepper

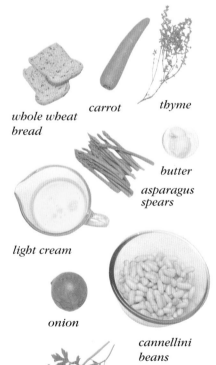

whole wheat bread *carrot* *thyme*

butter

asparagus spears

light cream

onion

cannellini beans

parsley

1 Melt the butter in a pan. Add the onion and carrot, and fry over a moderate heat for 4 minutes until soft. Add the thyme leaves.

2 Rinse the cannellini beans under cold running water. Drain thoroughly. Then add to the onion and carrot. Mix lightly.

3 Pour in the cream, and heat slowly to just below boiling point, stirring occasionally. Remove the pan from the heat, and add salt and pepper to taste. Preheat the broiler.

4 Place the asparagus spears in a saucepan. Pour over just enough boiling water to cover. Poach for 3–4 minutes until the spears are just tender.

5 Meanwhile, toast the bread under the broiler until both sides are golden.

6 Place the toast on individual plates. Drain the asparagus, and divide the spears between the slices of toast. Spoon the bean mixture over each portion, and serve.

Red Fried Rice

This vibrant rice dish owes its appeal as much to the bright colors of red onion, red bell pepper and tomatoes as it does to their flavors.

Serves 2

INGREDIENTS
¾ cup basmati rice
2 tbsp peanut oil
1 small red onion, chopped
1 red bell pepper, seeded and
  chopped
8 oz cherry tomatoes, halved
2 eggs, beaten
salt and freshly ground black pepper

eggs

basmati rice

cherry
tomatoes

red onion

red bell
pepper

1 Wash the rice several times under cold running water. Drain well. Bring a large pan of water to a boil. Add the rice, and cook for 10–12 minutes.

2 Meanwhile, heat the oil in a wok until very hot. Add the onion and red pepper, and stir-fry for 2–3 minutes. Add the cherry tomatoes, and stir-fry for 2 minutes more.

3 Pour in the beaten eggs all at once. Cook for 30 seconds without stirring, then stir to break up the egg as it sets.

4 Drain the cooked rice thoroughly. Add to the wok, and toss it over the heat with the vegetable and egg mixture for 3 minutes. Season the fried rice with salt and pepper to taste.

Chick-pea Stew

This hearty chick-pea and vegetable stew makes a filling meal. It is delicious served with garlic-flavored mashed potatoes.

Serves 4

INGREDIENTS

2 tbsp olive oil
1 small onion, chopped
8 oz carrots, halved lengthwise
  and thinly sliced
½ tsp ground cumin
1 tsp ground coriander
2 tbsp all-purpose flour
8 oz zucchini, sliced
7 oz can corn, drained
14 oz can chick-peas, drained
2 tbsp tomato paste
scant 1 cup hot vegetable bouillon,
  made from a cube
salt and freshly ground black pepper

onion   tomato
             paste

corn   chick-peas

             bouillon
             cube

ground
cumin

             carrots

ground
coriander

all-purpose
flour   zucchini

1 Heat the oil in a frying pan. Add the onion and carrots. Toss to coat the vegetables in the oil. Then cook over moderate heat for 4 minutes.

2 Add the ground cumin, coriander and flour. Stir, and cook for 1 minute.

COOK'S TIP

For speedy garlic-flavored mashed potatoes, simply mash potatoes with garlic butter and stir in chopped fresh parsley and a little sour cream.

3 Cut the zucchini slices in half., then add them to the pan with the corn, chick-peas, tomato paste and vegetable bouillon. Stir well. Cook gently for 10 minutes, stirring frequently.

4 Taste the stew, and add salt and pepper. Serve at once, with garlic-flavored mashed potatoes (see Cook's Tip), if desired.

Eggplant Pilaf

This hearty dish is made with bulgur and eggplant, flavored with fresh mint.

Serves 2

INGREDIENTS

2 eggplants
4–6 tbsp sunflower oil
1 small onion, finely chopped
1 cup bulgur
scant 2 cups vegetable bouillon,
  made from a cube
2 tbsp pine nuts, toasted
1 tbsp chopped fresh mint
salt and freshly ground black pepper

FOR THE GARNISH
lime wedges
lemon wedges
torn mint leaves

mint

pine nuts

bouillon cube

bulgur

onion

eggplants

COOK'S TIP

To cut down on the cooking time, soak the bulgur in water to cover by 1 in for up to 8 hours. Drain, and then continue as described in the recipe below, reducing the cooking time to just 8 minutes.

1 Remove the ends from the eggplants. Using a sharp knife, cut them into neat sticks and then into ¹/₂ in dice.

2 Heat 4 tbsp of the oil in a large frying pan. Add the onion, and sauté for 1 minute.

3 Add the diced eggplants. Cook over a high heat, stirring frequently, for about 4 minutes until just tender. Add the remaining oil, if needed.

4 Stir in the bulgur, mixing well. Then pour in the vegetable bouillon. Bring to a boil. Then lower the heat, and simmer for 10 minutes or until all the liquid has evaporated. Season to taste.

5 Add the pine nuts, and stir gently with a wooden spoon. Stir in the mint.

6 Spoon the pilaf on to individual plates, and garnish each portion with lime and lemon wedges. Sprinkle with torn mint leaves for extra color.

Hummus with Pan-fried Zucchini

Pan-fried zucchini are perfect for dipping into homemade hummus.

Serves 4

INGREDIENTS
8 oz can chick-peas
2 garlic cloves, coarsely chopped
6 tbsp lemon juice
4 tbsp tahini
5 tbsp olive oil, plus extra to serve
1 tsp ground cumin
1 lb small zucchini
salt and freshly ground black pepper

TO SERVE
paprika
pita bread
black olives

zucchini

chick peas   lemon

tahini

garlic cloves

ground
cumin

1 Drain the chick-peas, reserving the liquid from the can, and turn them into a food processor or blender. Blend to a smooth paste, adding a small amount of the reserved liquid, if necessary.

2 Mix the garlic, lemon juice and tahini together, and add to the food processor or blender. Process until smooth. With the machine running, gradually add 3 tbsp of the olive oil through the feeder tube or lid.

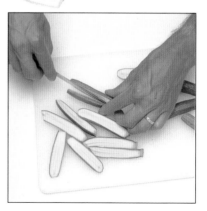

3 Add the cumin, with salt and pepper to taste. Process to mix. Then scrape the hummus into a bowl. Cover, and chill until required.

4 Remove the ends from the zucchini. Slice the zucchini lengthwise into even-size pieces.

5 Heat the remaining oil in a large frying pan. Season the zucchini, and fry them for 2–3 minutes on each side until just tender.

COOK'S TIP
Hummus is also delicious served with pan-fried or broiled eggplant slices.

6 Divide the zucchini among four individual plates. Spoon a portion of hummus on to each plate, and sprinkle with paprika. Add two or three pieces of sliced pita bread, and serve with olives.

Lentil Stir-fry

Mushrooms, artichokes, sugar snap peas and lentils make a satisfying stir-fry supper.

Serves 2–3

INGREDIENTS
4 oz sugar snap peas
1 oz butter
1 small onion, chopped
4 oz cup or button mushrooms,
 sliced
14 oz can artichoke hearts,
 drained and halved
14 oz can green lentils, drained
4 tbsp light cream
¼ cup shaved almonds, toasted
salt and freshly ground black pepper
French bread, to serve

light cream

green lentils

cup mushrooms

sugar snap peas

shaved almonds

artichoke hearts

onion

COOK'S TIP
Use strained, plain yogurt instead of the cream, if you like.

1 Bring a pan of salted water to a boil. Add the sugar snap peas, and cook for about 4 minutes until just tender. Drain, and refresh under cold running water. Then drain again. Pat dry the peas with paper towels, and set aside.

2 Melt the butter in a frying pan. Add the chopped onion and cook for 2–3 minutes, stirring occasionally.

3 Add the sliced mushrooms to the onion. Stir until combined. Then cook for 2–3 minutes until just tender. Add the artichokes, sugar snap peas and lentils to the pan. Stir-fry for 2 minutes.

4 Stir in the cream and almonds, and cook for 1 minute. Season to taste. Serve at once, with chunks of French bread.

Nut Pilaf with Omelet Rolls

A wonderful mixture of textures – soft, fluffy rice with crunchy nuts and omelet rolls.

Serves 2

INGREDIENTS
1 cup basmati rice
1 tbsp sunflower oil
1 small onion, chopped
1 red bell pepper, finely diced
1½ cups hot vegetable bouillon,
  made from a cube
2 eggs
¼ cup salted peanuts
1 tbsp soy sauce
salt and freshly ground black pepper
parsley sprigs, to garnish

salted peanuts

parsley

onion

eggs

bouillon cube

red bell pepper

basmati rice

1 Wash the rice several times under cold running water. Drain thoroughly. Heat half the oil in a large frying pan. Fry the onion and bell pepper for 2–3 minutes. Then stir in the rice and bouillon. Bring to a boil, and cook for 10 minutes until the rice is tender.

2 Meanwhile, beat the eggs lightly with salt and pepper to taste. Heat the remaining oil in a second large frying pan. Pour in the eggs, and tilt the pan to cover the base thinly. Cook the omelet for 1 minute. Then flip it over, and cook the other side for 1 minute.

3 Carefully slide the omelet on to a clean board, and roll it up tightly. Cut the omelet roll into eight slices.

4 Stir the peanuts and soy sauce into the pilaf, and add black pepper to taste. Turn the pilaf into a serving dish. Arrange the omelet rolls on top, and garnish with the parsley. Serve at once.

Kedgeree with Green Beans and Mushrooms

Crunchy green beans and mushrooms are the star ingredients in this vegetarian version of an old favorite.

Serves 2

INGREDIENTS

¾ cup basmati rice
1¼ cups cold water
3 eggs
6 oz green beans, trimmed
¼ cup butter
1 onion, finely chopped
8 oz crimini mushrooms, quartered
2 tbsp light cream
1 tbsp chopped fresh parsley
salt and freshly ground black pepper

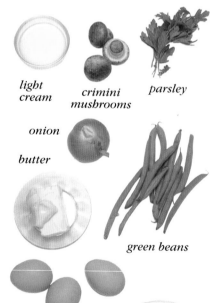

light cream

crimini mushrooms

parsley

onion

butter

green beans

eggs

basmati rice

1 Wash the rice several times under cold running water. Drain thoroughly. Bring a pan of water to a boil. Add the rice, and cook for 10–12 minutes until tender. Drain thoroughly.

2 Half fill a second pan with water. Add the eggs, and bring to a boil. Lower the heat, and simmer for 8 minutes. Drain the eggs, and cool them under cold water. Remove the shells.

3 Bring another pan of water to a boil, and cook the green beans for 5 minutes. Drain, and refresh under cold running water. Then drain again.

4 Melt the butter in a large frying pan. Add the onions and mushrooms. Cook for 2–3 minutes over a moderate heat.

5 Add the green beans and rice to the onion mixture. Stir lightly to mix. Cook for 2 minutes. Cut the hard-boiled eggs in wedges, and add them to the pan.

6 Stir in the cream and parsley, taking care not to break up the eggs. Reheat the kedgeree, but do not allow it to boil. Serve at once.

Chick-pea Falafel with Cilantro Dip

Little balls of spicy chick-pea purée, deep-fried until crisp, are served together with a cilantro-flavored mayonnaise.

Serves 4

INGREDIENTS
14 oz can chick-peas, drained
6 scallions, finely sliced
1 egg
1/2 tsp ground turmeric
1 garlic clove, crushed
1 tsp ground cumin
4 tbsp chopped fresh cilantro
oil for deep-frying
1 small red chili, seeded and
　finely chopped
3 tbsp mayonnaise
salt and freshly ground black pepper
cilantro sprig, to garnish

cilantro

scallions

chick-peas

ground
turmeric

ground
cumin

egg

garlic
clove

red
chili

mayonnaise

COOK'S TIP
If you have time, chill the chick-pea purée before making it into balls. It will be easier to shape.

1 Turn the chick-peas into a food processor or blender. Add the scallions, and process to a smooth purée. Add the egg, ground turmeric, garlic, cumin and about 1 tbsp of the chopped cilantro. Process briefly to mix, then add salt and pepper to taste.

2 Working with clean, wet hands, shape the chick-pea mixture into about sixteen small balls.

3 Heat the oil for deep-frying to 350°F or until a cube of bread, when added to the oil, browns in 30–45 seconds. Deep-fry the falafel in batches for 2–3 minutes or until golden. Drain on paper towels. Then place in a serving bowl.

4 Stir the remaining cilantro and the chili into the mayonnaise. Garnish with the cilantro sprig, and serve alongside the falafel.

Three Bean Salad with Yogurt Dressing

This tangy bean and pasta salad is great on its own or can be served as a side dish.

Serves 3–4

INGREDIENTS

3 oz penne or other dried
  pasta shapes
2 tomatoes
7 oz canned red kidney beans,
  drained
7 oz canned cannellini beans,
  drained
7 oz canned chick-peas, drained
1 green bell pepper, seeded and
  diced
3 tbsp plain yogurt
2 tbsp sunflower oil
grated rind of ¹/₂ lemon
2 tsp whole-grain mustard
1 tsp chopped fresh oregano
salt and freshly ground black pepper

penne

oregano

green bell pepper

red kidney beans

cannellini beans

plain yogurt

chick-peas

lemon

whole-grain mustard

tomatoes

1 Bring a large pan of salted water to a boil. Add the pasta, and cook for 10–12 minutes until just tender. Drain. Cool under cold water, and drain again.

2 Make a cross with the tip of a sharp knife in each of the tomatoes. Plunge them into a bowl of boiling water for 30 seconds. Remove with a slotted spoon or spatula, run under cold water, and peel away the skins. Cut the tomatoes into segments.

3 Drain the canned beans and chick-peas in a colander. Rinse them under cold water, and drain again. Turn into a bowl. Add the tomato segments, green bell pepper and pasta.

4 Whisk the yogurt until smooth. Gradually whisk in the oil, lemon rind and mustard. Stir in the oregano and salt and pepper to taste. Pour the dressing over the salad, and toss well.

Pumpkin and Pistachio Risotto

This elegant combination of creamy golden rice and orange pumpkin can be as pale or bright as you like by adding different quantities of saffron.

Serves 4

INGREDIENTS

5 cups fresh vegetable stock or water
generous pinch of saffron threads
2 tbsp olive oil
1 medium onion, chopped
2 garlic cloves, crushed
1 lb arborio rice
2 lb pumpkin, peeled, seeded and cut
    into ¾ in cubes
¾ cup dry white wine
½ oz Parmesan cheese, finely grated
½ cup pistachios
3 tbsp chopped fresh marjoram or
    oregano, plus extra leaves, to
    garnish
salt, freshly grated nutmeg and ground
    black pepper

2 Heat the oil in a large saucepan. Add the onion and garlic and cook gently for about 5 minutes until softened. Add the rice and pumpkin and cook for a few more minutes until the rice looks transparent.

3 Pour in the wine and allow it to boil hard. When it is absorbed add ¼ of the stock and the infused saffron and liquid. Stir constantly until all the liquid is absorbed.

1 Bring the stock or water to a boil and reduce to a low simmer. Ladle a little stock into a small bowl. Add the saffron threads and leave to infuse.

4 Gradually add the stock or water, a ladleful at a time, allowing the rice to absorb the liquid before adding more and stirring all the time. After 20–30 minutes the rice should be golden yellow and creamy, and *al dente* when tested.

saffron

pumpkin

white wine

onion

garlic

marjoram

Parmesan

arborio rice

pistachios

5 Stir in the Parmesan cheese, cover the pan and leave to stand for 5 minutes.

6 To finish, stir in the pistachios and marjoram or oregano. Season to taste with a little salt, nutmeg and pepper, and scatter over a few extra marjoram or oregano leaves.

COOK'S TIP
Italian arborio rice must be used to make an authentic risotto. Choose unpolished white arborio as it contains more starch.

Wild Rice Rösti with Carrot and Orange Purée

Rösti is a traditional dish from Switzerland. This variation has the extra nuttiness of wild rice and a bright simple sauce as a fresh accompaniment.

Serves 6

INGREDIENTS
½ cup wild rice
2 lb large potatoes
3 tbsp walnut oil
1 tsp yellow mustard seeds
1 onion, coarsely grated and drained in a sieve
2 tbsp fresh thyme leaves
salt and freshly ground black pepper

FOR THE PURÉE
12 oz carrots, peeled and roughly chopped
rind and juice of 1 large orange

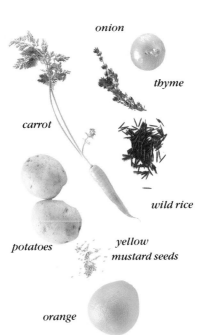

onion

thyme

carrot

wild rice

potatoes

yellow mustard seeds

orange

1 For the purée, place the carrots in a pan, cover with cold water and add 2 pieces of orange rind. Bring to a boil and cook for 10 minutes or until tender. Drain well and discard the rind.

2 Purée the mixture in a blender with 4 tbsp of the orange juice. Return to the pan to reheat.

3 Place the wild rice in a clean pan and cover with water. Bring to a boil and cook for 30–40 minutes, until the rice is just starting to split, but still crunchy. Drain the rice.

4 Scrub the potatoes, place in a large pan and cover with cold water. Bring to a boil and cook for 10–15 minutes until just tender. Drain well and leave to cool slightly. When the potatoes are cool, peel and coarsely grate them into a large bowl. Add the cooked rice.

5 Heat 2 tbsp of the walnut oil in a non-stick frying pan and add the mustard seeds. When they start to pop, add the onion and cook gently for 5 minutes until softened. Add to the bowl of potato and rice, together with the thyme, and mix thoroughly. Season to taste with salt and pepper.

6 Heat the remaining oil in the frying pan and add the potato mixture. Press down well and cook for 10 minutes or until golden brown. Cover the pan with a plate and flip over, then slide the rösti back into the pan for another 10 minutes to cook the other side. Serve with the reheated carrot and orange purée.

Thai Fragrant Rice

A lovely, soft, fluffy rice dish, perfumed with fresh lemon grass.

Serves 4

INGREDIENTS
1 piece of lemon grass
2 limes
1 cup brown basmati rice
1 tbsp olive oil
1 onion, chopped
1 in piece of fresh ginger root, peeled and finely chopped
1½ tsp coriander seeds
1½ tsp cumin seeds
3 cups fresh vegetable stock or water
4 tbsp chopped fresh coriander
lime wedges, to serve

onion

ginger

lime

lemon grass

coriander seeds

basmati rice

cumin seeds

coriander

1 Finely chop the lemon grass.

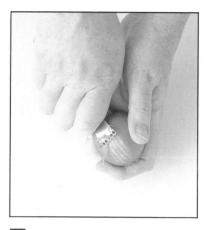

2 Remove the zest from the limes using a zester or fine grater.

3 Rinse the rice in plenty of cold water until the water runs clear. Drain through a sieve.

4 Heat the oil in a large pan and add the onion and spices, lemon grass and lime zest and cook gently for 2–3 minutes.

5 Add the rice and cook for another minute, then add the stock and bring to a boil. Reduce the heat to very low and cover the pan. Cook gently for 30 minutes then check the rice. If it is still crunchy, cover the pan again and leave for a further 3–5 minutes. Remove from the heat.

6 Stir in the fresh coriander, fluff up the grains, cover and leave for 10 minutes. Serve with lime wedges.

COOK'S TIP

Other varieties of rice, such as white basmati or long grain, can be used for this dish but you will need to adjust the cooking times accordingly.

Cannellini Bean Purée with Grilled Radicchio

The slightly bitter flavors of the radicchio and chicory make a wonderful marriage with the creamy citrus flavored bean purée.

Serves 4

INGREDIENTS
14 oz can cannellini beans
3 tbsp low-fat ricotta cheese
finely grated rind and juice of 1
  large orange
1 tbsp finely chopped fresh rosemary
4 heads of chicory
2 medium radicchio
1 tbsp walnut oil

chicory

ricotta cheese

cannellini
beans

rosemary

radicchio

orange

1 Drain the beans, rinse, and drain again. Purée the beans in a blender or food processor with the ricotta cheese, orange juice and rosemary. Set aside.

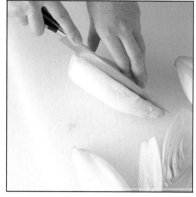

2 Cut the chicory in half lengthwise.

3 Cut each radicchio into 8 wedges.

4 Lay out the chicory and radicchio on a baking tray and brush with walnut oil. Grill for 2–3 minutes. Serve with the sauce and scatter over the orange rind.

COOK'S TIP

Other suitable beans to use are navy, mung or broad beans.

Tabouli with Fennel and Pomegranate

A fresh salad originating in the Middle East, with the added crunchiness of fennel and sweet pomegranate seeds. It is perfect for a summer lunch.

Serves 6

INGREDIENTS

1 cup bulgur wheat
2 fennel bulbs
1 small fresh red chilli, seeded and finely chopped
1 celery stalk, finely sliced
30 ml/2 tbsp olive oil
finely grated rind and juice of 2 lemons
6–8 scallions, chopped
6 tbsp chopped fresh mint
6 tbsp chopped fresh parsley
1 pomegranate, seeds removed
salt and freshly ground black pepper

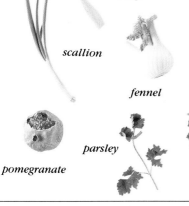

lemon

red chilli

celery

bulgur wheat

scallion

fennel

pomegranate

parsley

mint

1 Place the bulgur wheat in a bowl and pour over enough cold water to cover. Leave to stand for 30 minutes.

2 Drain the wheat through a sieve, pressing out any excess water using a spoon.

3 Halve the fennel bulbs and cut into very fine slices.

4 Mix all the remaining ingredients together, including the soaked bulgur wheat and fennel. Season well, cover, and set aside for 30 minutes before serving.

Sweet Vegetable Couscous

A wonderful combination of sweet vegetables and spices, this makes a substantial winter dish.

Serves 4–6

INGREDIENTS

1 generous pinch of saffron threads
3 tbsp boiling water
1 tbsp olive oil
1 red onion, sliced
2 garlic, cloves
1–2 fresh red chillies, seeded and
　finely chopped
½ tsp ground ginger
½ tsp ground cinnamon
1 × 400 g/14 oz can chopped
　tomatoes
1¼ cups fresh vegetable stock or
　water
4 medium carrots, peeled and cut into
　¼ in slices
2 medium turnips, peeled and cut into
　¾ in cubes
1 lb sweet potatoes, peeled and cut
　into ¾ in cubes
⅓ cup raisins
2 medium zucchini, cut into ¼ in
　slices
1 × 14 oz can chick-peas, drained and
　rinsed
3 tbsp chopped fresh parsley
3 tbsp chopped fresh coriander
1 lb quick-cooking couscous

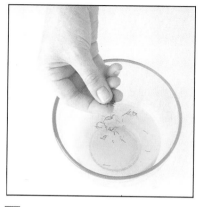

1 Leave the saffron to infuse in the boiling water.

2 Heat the oil in a large saucepan. Add the onion, garlic and chillies and cook gently for 5 minutes.

3 Add the ground ginger and cinnamon and cook for a further 1–2 minutes.

4 Add the tomatoes, stock or water, infused saffron and liquid, carrots, turnips, sweet potatoes and raisins, cover and simmer for 25 minutes.

red onion

chick-peas

couscous

chopped tomatoes

zucchini

carrot

red chilli

garlic

turnip

raisins

sweet potato

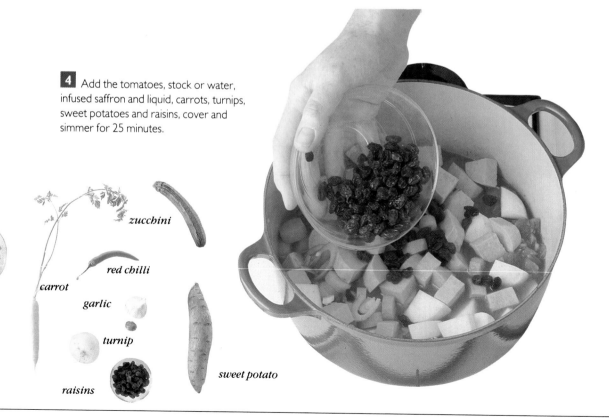

5 Add the zucchini, chick-peas, parsley and coriander and cook for another 10 minutes.

6 Meanwhile prepare the couscous following the package instructions and serve with the vegetables.

Lemon and Ginger Spicy Beans

An extremely quick delicious meal, made with canned beans for speed. You probably won't need extra salt as canned beans tend to be already salted.

Serves 4

INGREDIENTS
2 tbsp roughly chopped fresh ginger
    root
3 garlic cloves, roughly chopped
1 cup cold water
1 tbsp sunflower oil
1 large onion, thinly sliced
1 fresh red chilli, seeded and finely
    chopped
¼ tsp cayenne pepper
2 tsp ground cumin
1 tsp ground coriander
½ tsp ground turmeric
2 tbsp lemon juice
⅓ cup chopped fresh coriander
1 × 14 oz can black-eyed beans,
    drained and rinsed
1 × 14 oz can adzuki beans, drained
    and rinsed
1 × 14 oz can navy beans, drained and
    rinsed
freshly ground black pepper

garlic
red chilli
adzuki beans
ginger
black-eyed beans
ground coriander
ground turmeric
ground cumin
navy beans
onion

1 Place the ginger, garlic and 4 tbsp of the cold water in a blender and mix until smooth.

2 Heat the oil in a pan. Add the onion and chilli and cook gently for 5 minutes until softened.

3 Add the cayenne pepper, cumin, ground coriander and turmeric and stir-fry for 1 minute.

4 Stir in the ginger and garlic paste from the blender and cook for another minute.

5 Add the remaining water, lemon juice and fresh coriander, stir well and bring to a boil. Cover the pan tightly and cook for 5 minutes.

6 Add all the beans and cook for a further 5–10 minutes. Season with pepper to taste and serve.

Green Lentil and Cabbage Salad

This warm crunchy salad makes a satisfying meal if served with crusty French bread or wholemeal rolls.

Serves 4–6

INGREDIENTS
1 cup green lentils
6 cups cold water
1 garlic clove
1 bay leaf
1 small onion, peeled and studded
  with 2 cloves
1 tbsp olive oil
1 red onion, finely sliced
2 garlic cloves, crushed
1 tbsp thyme leaves
12 oz cabbage, finely shredded
finely grated rind and juice of 1 lemon
1 tbsp raspberry vinegar
salt and freshly ground black pepper

thyme

cabbage

onion

red onion

bay leaf

lemon

garlic

cloves

peppercorns

1 Rinse the lentils in cold water and place in a large pan with the water, peeled garlic clove, bay leaf and clove-studded onion. Bring to a boil and cook for 10 minutes. Reduce the heat, cover the pan and simmer gently for 15–20 minutes. Drain and remove the onion, garlic and bay leaf.

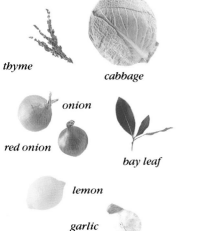

2 Heat the oil in a large pan. Add the red onion, garlic and thyme and cook for 5 minutes until softened.

3 Add the cabbage and cook for 3–5 minutes until just cooked but still crunchy.

4 Stir in the cooked lentils, lemon rind and juice and the raspberry vinegar. Season to taste and serve.

Polenta and Baked Tomatoes

A staple of northern Italy, polenta is a nourishing, filling food, served here with a delicious fresh tomato and olive topping.

Serves 4–6

INGREDIENTS
9 cups water
1¼ lb quick-cooking polenta
12 large ripe plum tomatoes, sliced
4 garlic cloves, thinly sliced
2 tbsp chopped fresh oregano or
    marjoram
½ cup black olives, pitted
salt and freshly ground black pepper
2 tbsp olive oil

black olives

marjoram

plum
tomatoes

garlic

oregano

polenta

1 Place the water in a large saucepan and bring to a boil. Whisk in the polenta and simmer for 5 minutes.

2 Remove the pan from the heat and pour the thickened polenta into a 9 in × 13 in jelly roll pan. Smooth out the surface with a spatula until level, and leave to cool.

3 Preheat the oven to 350°F. With a 3 in round pastry cutter, stamp out 12 rounds of polenta. Lay them so that they slightly overlap in a lightly oiled ovenproof dish.

4 Layer the tomatoes, garlic, oregano or marjoram and olives on top of the polenta, seasoning the layers as you go. Sprinkle with the olive oil, and bake uncovered for 30–35 minutes. Serve immediately.

French Bread Pizzas with Artichokes

Crunchy French bread makes an ideal base for these quick pizzas.

Serves 4

INGREDIENTS
1 tbsp sunflower oil
1 onion, chopped
1 green bell pepper, seeded and
  chopped
7 oz can chopped tomatoes
1 tbsp tomato paste
1/2 French stick
14 oz can artichoke hearts, drained
4 oz mozzarella cheese, sliced
1 tbsp poppy seeds
salt and freshly ground black pepper

mozzarella cheese

French stick

tomato paste

chopped tomatoes

green bell pepper

poppy seeds

onion

artichoke hearts

1 Heat the oil in a frying pan. Add the chopped onion and bell pepper, and cook for 4 minutes until just softened.

2 Stir in the chopped tomatoes and tomato paste. Cook for 4 minutes. Remove from the heat, and add salt and pepper to taste.

3 Cut the piece of French stick in half lengthwise. Cut each half in four to give eight pieces in all.

4 Spoon a little of the pepper and tomato mixture over each piece of bread. Preheat the broiler.

5 Slice the artichoke hearts. Arrange them on top of the pepper and tomato mixture. Cover with the mozzarella slices, and sprinkle with the poppy seeds.

6 Arrange the French bread pizzas on a rack over a broiler pan, and broil for 6–8 minutes until the cheese melts and is beginning to brown. Serve at once.

Zucchini and Walnut Loaf

Cardamom seeds impart their distinctive aroma to this loaf. Serve spread with ricotta and honey for a delicious snack.

Makes 1 loaf

INGREDIENTS
3 eggs
⅓ cup light brown sugar, firmly
    packed
½ cup sunflower oil
2 cups wholewheat flour
1 tsp baking powder
1 tsp baking soda
1 tsp ground cinnamon
¾ tsp ground allspice
½ tbsp green cardamoms, seeds
    removed and crushed
5 oz zucchini, coarsely grated
½ cup walnuts, chopped
¼ cup sunflower seeds

zucchini

walnuts

egg

sunflower oil

brown sugar

wholewheat flour

sunflower seeds

cardamom pods

1 Preheat the oven to 350°F. Line the base and sides of a 2 lb loaf pan with parchment paper.

2 Beat the eggs and sugar together and gradually add the oil.

3 Sift the flour into a bowl together with the baking powder, baking soda, cinnamon and allspice.

4 Mix into the egg mixture with the rest of the ingredients, reserving 1 tbsp of the sunflower seeds for the top.

5 Spoon into the loaf tin, level off the top, and sprinkle with the reserved sunflower seeds.

6 Bake for 1 hour or until a skewer inserted in the center comes out clean. Leave to cool slightly before turning out onto a wire rack to cool completely.

Red Pepper and Watercress Filo Parcels

Peppery watercress combines well with sweet red pepper in these crisp little parcels.

Makes 8

INGREDIENTS
3 red peppers
6 oz watercress
1 cup ricotta cheese
¼ cup blanched almonds, toasted and chopped
salt and freshly ground black pepper
8 sheets of filo pastry
2 tbsp olive oil

ricotta

red pepper

watercress

almonds

filo pastry

1 Preheat the oven to 375°F. Place the peppers under a hot broiler until blistered and charred. Place in a paper bag. When cool enough to handle peel, seed and pat dry on kitchen paper.

2 Place the peppers and watercress in a food processor and pulse until coarsely chopped. Spoon into a bowl.

3 Mix in the ricotta and almonds, and season to taste.

4 Working with 1 sheet of filo pastry at a time, cut out 2 × 7 in and 2 × 2 in squares from each sheet. Brush 1 large square with a little olive oil and place a second large square at an angle of 90 degrees to form a star shape.

5 Place 1 of the small squares in the center of the star shape, brush lightly with oil and top with a second small square.

6 Top with ⅛ of the red pepper mixture. Bring the edges together to form a purse shape and twist to seal. Place on a lightly greased cookie sheet and cook for 25–30 minutes until golden.

Sage Soda Bread

This wonderful loaf, quite unlike bread made with yeast, has a velvety texture and a powerful sage aroma.

Makes 1 loaf

INGREDIENTS
2 cups wholewheat flour
1 cup flour
½ tsp salt
1 tsp baking soda
2 tbsp shredded fresh sage or 2 tsp
    dried sage, crumbled
1¼–1¾ cups buttermilk

white flour

wholewheat flour

sage

buttermilk

COOK'S TIP

As an alternative to the sage, try using finely chopped rosemary or thyme.

1 Preheat the oven to 425°F. Sift the dry ingredients into a bowl.

2 Stir in the sage and add enough buttermilk to make a soft dough.

3 Shape the dough into a round loaf and place on a lightly oiled cookie sheet.

4 Cut a deep cross in the top. Bake in the oven for 40 minutes until the loaf is well risen and sounds hollow when tapped on the bottom. Leave to cool on a wire rack.

Mini Pizzas

For a quick supper dish try these delicious little pizzas made with fresh and sun-dried tomatoes.

Makes 4

INGREDIENTS
1 × 5 oz package pizza mix
8 halves sun-dried tomatoes in olive oil, drained
½ cup black olives, pitted
8 oz ripe tomatoes, sliced
¼ cup goat cheese
2 tbsp fresh basil leaves

basil

tomatoes

sun-dried tomatoes

black olives

goat cheese

1 Preheat the oven to 400°F. Make up the pizza base following the instructions on the side of the package.

2 Divide the dough into 4 and roll each piece out to a 5 in disc. Place on a lightly oiled cookie sheet.

3 Place the sun-dried tomatoes and olives in a blender or food processor and blend until smooth. Spread the mixture evenly over the pizza bases.

4 Top with the tomato slices and crumble over the goat cheese. Bake for 10–15 minutes. Sprinkle with the fresh basil and serve.

Eggplant, Shallot and Sun-dried Tomato Calzone

Eggplant, shallots and sun-dried tomatoes make an unusual filling for calzone. Add more or less red chili flakes, depending on personal taste.

Serves 2

INGREDIENTS
3 tbsp olive oil
3 shallots, chopped
4 baby eggplant
1 garlic clove, chopped
2 oz sun-dried tomatoes
  in oil, chopped
¼ tsp dried red chili flakes
2 tsp chopped fresh thyme
1 packet pizza dough mix
3 oz mozzarella, cubed
salt and ground black pepper
1–2 tbsp freshly grated
  Parmesan, to serve

Parmesan

thyme

mozzarella

olive oil

baby eggplants

shallots

red chili flakes

1 Preheat the oven to 425°F. Heat 2 tbsp of the oil in a frying pan. Add the shallots and cook until soft. Trim the eggplants, then cut into small cubes.

2 Add the eggplants to the shallots with the garlic, sun-dried tomatoes, red chili flakes, thyme and seasoning. Cook for 4–5 minutes, stirring frequently, until the eggplant is beginning to soften. Remove from the heat and let cool.

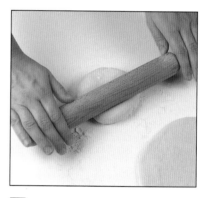

3 Make the dough according to the directions on the packet. Divide the dough in half and roll out each piece on a lightly floured surface to and 18 cm/7 in circle.

4 Spread the eggplant mixture over half of each circle, leaving a 1 in border, then scatter the mozzarella over.

5 Dampen the edges with water, then fold over the other half of dough to enclose the filling. Press the edges firmly together to seal. Place on two greased baking sheets.

6 Brush with half the remaining oil and make a small hole in the top of each to allow the steam to escape. Bake for 15–20 minutes until golden. Remove from the oven and brush with the remaining oil. Sprinkle the Parmesan over and serve immediately.

Parsnip and Pecan Cheese Puffs with Watercress and Arugula Sauce

These scrumptious nutty puffs conceal a surprisingly sweet parsnip center.

Makes 18

INGREDIENTS
½ cup butter
1¼ cups water
¾ cup plain flour
½ cup wholewheat flour
3 eggs, beaten
1 oz Cheddar cheese, grated
pinch of cayenne pepper or paprika
⅓ cup pecans, chopped
1 medium parsnip, cut into
    ¾ in pieces
1 tbsp skim milk
2 tsp sesame seeds

FOR THE SAUCE
5 oz watercress, trimmed
5 oz arugula, trimmed
¾ cup low-fat yogurt
salt, grated nutmeg and freshly ground
    black pepper
watercress sprigs, to garnish

2 Beat in the Cheddar, cayenne pepper or paprika and the chopped pecans.

pecans

Cheddar

parsnips

arugula

wholewheat flour

plain flour

egg

yogurt

watercress

1 Preheat the oven to 400°F. Place the butter and water in a pot. Bring to a boil and add all the flour at once. Beat vigorously until the mixture leaves the sides of the pan and forms a ball. Remove from heat and allow the mixture to cool slightly. Beat in the eggs a little at a time until the mixture is shiny and soft enough to fall gently from a spoon.

3 Lightly grease a cookie sheet and drop onto it 18 heaped tablespoons of the mixture. Place a piece of parsnip on each and top with another heaped tablespoon of the mixture.

4 Brush the puffs with a little milk and sprinkle with sesame seeds. Bake in the oven for 25–30 minutes until golden.

5 Meanwhile make the sauce. Bring a pan of water to a boil and blanch the watercress and arugula for 2–3 minutes. Drain and immediately refresh in cold water. Drain well and chop.

6 Purée the watercress and arugula in a blender or food processor with the yogurt until smooth. Season to taste with salt, nutmeg and freshly ground black pepper. To reheat, place the sauce in a bowl over a gently simmering pot of hot water and heat gently, taking care not to let the sauce curdle. Garnish with watercress.

Tomato Breadsticks

Once you've tried this simple recipe you'll never buy manufactured breadsticks again. Serve with aperitifs, with a dip or with cheese to end a meal.

Makes 16

INGREDIENTS
2 cups plain flour
½ tsp salt
½ tbsp easy-blend dry yeast
1 tsp honey
1 tsp olive oil
⅔ cup warm water
6 halves sun-dried tomatoes in olive oil, drained and chopped
1 tbsp skim milk
2 tsp poppy seeds

plain flour

sun-dried tomatoes

honey

yeast

poppy seeds

1 Place the flour, salt and yeast in a food processor. Add the honey and olive oil and, with the machine running, gradually pour in the water (you may not need it all as flours vary). Stop adding water as soon as the dough starts to cling together. Process for 1 minute more.

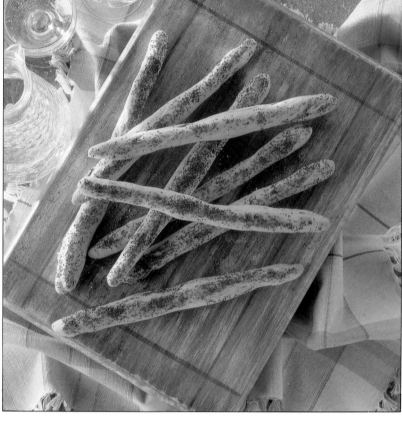

2 Turn out the dough onto a floured board and knead for 3–4 minutes until springy and smooth. Knead in the chopped sun-dried tomatoes. Form into a ball and place in a lightly oiled bowl. Leave to rise for 5 minutes.

3 Preheat the oven to 300°F. Divide the dough into 16 equal pieces and roll each piece into a 11 in × ½ in long stick. Place on a lightly oiled cookie sheet and leave to rise in a warm place for 15 minutes.

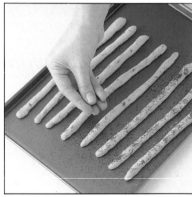

4 Brush the sticks with milk and sprinkle with poppy seeds. Bake for 30 minutes. Leave to cool on a wire rack.

Oatmeal Tartlets with Minted Hummus

Serve these wholesome little tartlets with a crisp salad of Boston lettuce.

Serves 6

INGREDIENTS
1½ cups medium oatmeal
½ tsp baking soda
1 tsp salt
2 tbsp butter
1 egg yolk
2 tbsp skim milk
1 × 14 oz can chick-peas, rinsed and
    drained
juice of 1–2 lemons
1½ cups ricotta cheese
4 tbsp tahini
freshly ground black pepper
3 tbsp chopped fresh mint
2 tbsp pumpkin seeds
paprika, for dusting

pumpkin seeds

tahini

ricotta cheese

chick-peas

oatmeal

mint

lemon

1 Preheat the oven to 325°F. Mix together the oatmeal, baking soda and salt in a large bowl. Rub in the butter until the mixture resembles fine breadcrumbs. Stir in the egg yolk and add the milk if the mixture seems too dry.

2 Press into 3½ in tartlet pans. Bake for 25–30 minutes. Allow to cool.

3 Purée the chick-peas, the juice of 1 lemon, ricotta cheese and tahini in a food processor until smooth. Spoon into a bowl and season with black pepper and more lemon juice to taste. Stir in the chopped mint. Divide between the tartlet moulds, sprinkle with pumpkin seeds and dust with paprika.

Saffron Focaccia

A dazzling yellow bread that is light in texture and distinctive in flavor.

Makes 1 loaf

INGREDIENTS
pinch of saffron threads
²⁄₃ cup boiling water
2 cups flour
½ tsp salt
1 tsp easy-blend dry yeast
1 tbsp olive oil

FOR THE TOPPING
2 garlic cloves, sliced
1 red onion, cut into thin wedges
rosemary sprigs
12 black olives, pitted and coarsely chopped
1 tbsp olive oil

flour

garlic

rosemary

red onion

olives

saffron

yeast

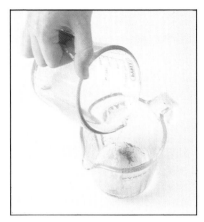

1 Place the saffron in a heatproof cup and pour on the boiling water. Leave to stand and infuse until lukewarm.

2 Place the flour, salt, yeast and olive oil in a food processor. Turn on and gradually add the saffron and its liquid. Process until the dough forms into a ball.

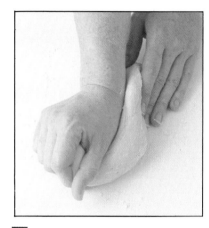

3 Turn onto a floured board and knead for 10–15 minutes. Place in a bowl, cover and leave to rise for 30–40 minutes until doubled in size.

4 Punch down the risen dough on a lightly floured surface and roll out into an oval shape, ½ in thick. Place on a lightly greased cookie sheet and leave to rise for 20–30 minutes.

5 Preheat the oven to 400°F. Press small indentations all over the surface of the focaccia with your fingers.

6 Cover with the topping ingredients, brush lightly with olive oil, and bake for 25 minutes or until the loaf sounds hollow when tapped on the bottom. Leave to cool on a wire rack.

Date and Apple Muffins

You'll only need one or two of these wholesome muffins per person, since they are very filling.

Makes 12

INGREDIENTS

1¼ cups self-rising whole-wheat
  flour
1¼ cups self-rising white flour
1 tsp ground cinnamon
1 tsp baking powder
2 tbsp margarine
½ cup light brown sugar
1 eating apple
1 cup apple juice
2 tbsp pear and apple spread
1 large egg, lightly beaten
½ cup chopped dates
1 tbsp chopped pecan halves

chopped dates   *egg*

pecans

self-rising whole-wheat flour

ground cinnamon

light brown sugar

self-rising white flour   *apple juice*

margarine

pear and apple spread

baking powder   *eating apple*

1 Preheat the oven to 400°F. Arrange twelve cupcake holders in a deep muffin pan. Put the whole-wheat flour in a mixing bowl. Sift in the white flour with the cinnamon and baking powder. Work in the margarine until the mixture resembles bread crumbs, then stir in the light brown sugar.

2 Quarter and core the apple, finely chop it, and set aside. Stir a little of the apple juice with the pear and apple spread until smooth. Stir in the remaining juice, then add to the flour mixture with the egg. Add the chopped apple to the bowl with the dates. Stir quickly until just combined.

3 Divide the batter evenly among the cupcake holders.

4 Sprinkle the muffins with the chopped pecan halves. Bake for about 20–25 minutes until golden brown and firm in the middle. Remove to a wire rack, and serve while still warm.

Raspberry Muffins

These muffins are made with baking powder and low fat buttermilk, giving them a light and spongy texture. They are delicious at any time of the day.

Makes 10–12

INGREDIENTS
2½ cups all-purpose flour
1 tbsp baking powder
½ cup sugar
1 large egg
1 cup buttermilk
4 tbsp sunflower oil
1 cup raspberries

egg

buttermilk

sunflower oil

sugar

flour

baking powder

raspberries

1 Preheat the oven to 400°F. Arrange twelve cupcake holders in a deep muffin pan. Sift the flour and baking powder into a mixing bowl, stir in the sugar, then make a well in the center.

2 Stir the egg, buttermilk and sunflower oil together in a bowl, pour into the flour mixture, and stir quickly until just combined.

3 Add the raspberries, and lightly fold them in with a metal spoon. Spoon the mixture into the cupcake holders, filling them two-thirds full.

4 Bake the muffins for 20–25 minutes until golden brown and firm in the middle. Transfer to a wire rack, and serve warm or cold.

INDEX

INDEX

INDEX

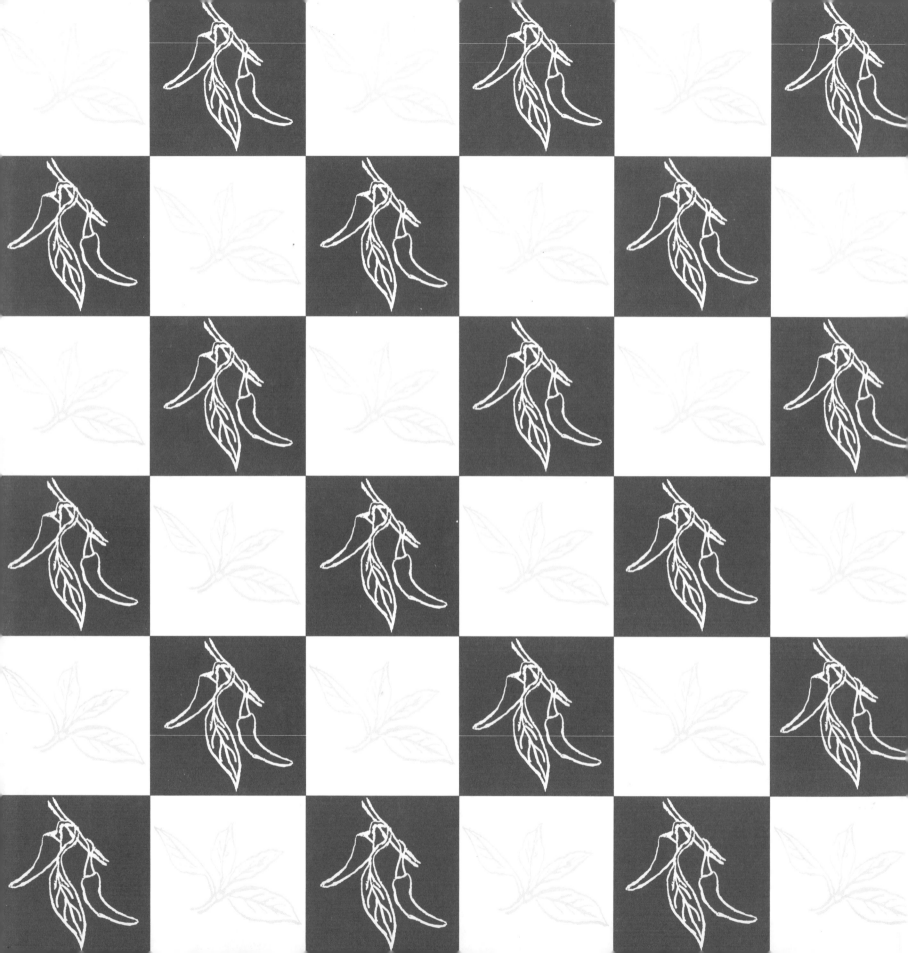